Co ing Military Medals

Collecting Military Medals

A Beginner's Guide

Colin Narbeth

The Lutterworth Press
Cambridge

Published by
The Lutterworth Press
P.O. Box 60
Cambridge
CB1 2NT
England

e-mail: **publishing@lutterworth.com**
website: **http://www.lutterworth.com**

ISBN 0 7188 9010 8 hardback
ISBN 0 7188 9009 4 paperback

British Library Cataloguing in Publication Data:
A catalogue record is available from the British Library.

First published 1971,
reprinted 2002

CONTENTS

LIST OF ILLUSTRATIONS

ACKNOWLEDGEMENTS

Of the many collectors and dealers who assisted the author, particular mention should be made of Mr David Paterson, a well-known collector, who checked many points and who compiled the index; Mr John Hayward of J. B. Hayward and Son, 17 Piccadilly Arcade, London S.W.1., one of the foremost medal dealers in the world, for supplying medals and ribbons for illustration; Mr D. M. Bolton of the London Stamp Exchange for permitting the author to have photographs taken of his display cases of medals and Putmans Photographers of Walton-on-Naze, Essex, who took many of the photographs.

INTRODUCTION

COLLECTING military medals has one tremendous appeal over all other collecting hobbies. Each medal has a personal history behind it and a great deal of the enjoyment obtained from medals is in unravelling that history. Naturally, it is not always possible to find out about the owner of a medal or what he did, but at least the collector starts with a vital clue—the man's name. The great majority of British campaign medals were 'named' and this means that more often than not the collector will find the recipient's name, rank and regiment or ship on the edge of the medal.

This facet of collecting is denied to the philatelist and numismatist and offers an alluring appeal to those who like the challenge of research of this nature.

Generally speaking, if a medal can be identified with an officer, then it is comparatively easy to find out about the man, his service career and what part he played in history. This is because the service careers of officers in HM Forces have been well docketed. Although nowhere so easy to trace, it is a practical proposition to try and find out about individual soldiers who took part in campaigns. The police, for example, would be most happy if someone would provide them with the name and whereabouts of criminals when they start their investigations. A medal in effect provides these valuable items of information. So, for those who like detective work, the challenge of finding out about the man behind the medal is by no means hopeless and depends upon individual thoroughness, persistence and, as with all things, a little luck!

Anyone with a few pounds to spare can start a medal collection, and those with large funds available can very quickly amass a large number of medals. Money is only one factor, however, and the true collector brings a collection to life and closes the generation gap between ourselves and our forefathers who marched to form one of the largest, and

1. *Long Service and Good Conduct Medal of King Edward VII's reign. The left-hand illustration shows the obverse ('head' side) and the right-hand shows the reverse ('tails' side). The condition of the medal and ribbon would be described as 'extremely fine'*

the longest-lasting empires in the history of the world. To him the finances for buying medals are only part of the equipment of the hobby. Money alone will not form an interesting medal collection (it may form a valuable one); only painstaking research and intelligent presentation will do this.

Not to be overlooked is the fact that the collector who searches and searches to find out about a soldier of the 93rd Foot who fought at Inkermann, and fails, has not wasted his time. The exercise will have taught him a great deal about the history of war and the endurance of men. If he has researched all possible channels, then by the time he has finished he will be a walking encyclopaedia on that particular battle— incidentally, this was the last battle in history where massed formations of fighting men met head-on with rifle butt, spade and fist.

The study of military history is the study of history. All war stems from politics—stems from the day the politicians fail to get what they want by talking. Once war starts a nation's resources are thrust behind it; suddenly improvisation necessitates new invention and, once the war is over, more often than not it leaves a legacy of progress in general civilization as well as in improved methods of destruction. The rapid development of radar in World War II was later to find even greater uses in peacetime, guiding fishing fleets, etc. The student of war medals absorbs all this knowledge, and there is no better springboard to future progress than a thorough appreciation of the past. Man's insensitivity to the past has often led to the repetition of mistakes.

Just how important history is can be illustrated by the fact that whenever we judge anything our criteria can only be what has happened before. Nothing can so fit a man to lead others than a thorough knowledge of history—a knowledge of what has happened before. The medal collector is gaining this knowledge of history all the time and is going further than the general student of history. He is making it breathe again. Some collecting hobbies can be criticized because although they stimulate the mind and bring happiness they do not of themselves necessarily serve a useful purpose.

This cannot be said of the medal collector. His is a truly useful pastime. As well as stimulation and enjoyment, he is improving his mind with the knowledge which can be put to practical purposes, and, on a purely nostalgic note, he is preserving the memory of the millions of men before him who each in his way took a hand in shaping our inheritance.

How different the shape of history would have been if the British fleet had been sunk at Trafalgar, if the Allies had fled at Waterloo! It is part of everyone's education in modern society to learn what happened at such events; the medal collector is not content to leave it at that, he wants to know who did it, and how.

It is not necessary to have a large collection of medals to relate history—even a dozen medals can give an interesting account of a regiment over a hundred years or more. Almost as important as the medals to the collector is his library. If funds do not permit a comprehensive library at home then the collector has at his disposal the public libraries which are always useful and which can very often trace obscure books which the collector needs for reference.

There are few specialist medal collectors who do not have extensive libraries of their own. In studying the medals of one regiment the collector may amass newspaper cuttings of the period relating to the regiment, letters written home by soldiers in the field, regimental histories and obscure references to the subject in biographies, etc. He is collating scraps of information from unusual sources to build up a full picture of the study he is making. He can bring to light 'forgotten' knowledge and add new snippets of information to enlarge the general knowledge of the events.

This is why sooner or later it is necessary to specialize. The man who just buys medals as and when they come his way ends up with a vast number of medals and little else. If he wants to know something about his medals he must contain his collection within reasonable limits, permitting him to make a close study of them. The man who can show you a hundred medals, but doesn't even know if a man's name is engraved or impressed on the edges is not a true collector; he is a medal amasser. If he takes so little interest in his medals the chances are that he does not even know if they are genuine or not.

The specialist, apart from being in a position to make a deep study of his chosen field, has the advantage of developing the ability to sense that something is wrong when he meets with a forgery. He will, with experience, know how the name of a person should appear on a medal of the particular group he is collecting; he will know that a certain military bar could not have been obtained in association with another, knowledge which a general collector would find impossible to absorb; and he will probably be able to turn up his records or even have a copy of the regiment's medal roll to ascertain whether a man was entitled to particular bars.

It is far better to specialize, enabling the collector to know what to expect to find and what it should look like. Anyone with enough money can buy lots of medals. It takes real collecting ability to acquire ten medals relating to the same warship for different actions it fought in. And once put together and studied those ten medals will tell a graphic history of that ship; a hundred varied medals, ranging from masonic or campaign medals to coronation or jubilee medals, will tell you nothing other than that such medals were issued.

There is a breed of collector whose enthusiasm in collecting is such that he finds it very difficult to resist obtaining items which take his fancy, even though they do not relate to his subject. Often the sudden enthusiasm wanes when it is realized how useless the item is to the study being made—but, then it is too late and the money has been spent. This impulsive purchasing is not nearly so rare as some would believe. The experienced collector will have disciplined himself to be more selective, even if only by bitter experience. The new collector could do a lot worse than to start a file for each new medal he acquires and make a point of not getting any more until he has found out something about that medal to put in his file. Naturally, one is referring to general additions to a collection—exceptions would be outright bargains or medals which fit into the general pattern of a specialized study and which may not be easy to find again if not taken at once.

Before spending large sums of money on rare medals the collector should be conversant with known forgeries and methods of doctoring medals. There is no substitute for experience and the sensible collector starts off with the more readily available material from which he gains the knowledge which enables him to spend out on rarities, which in some instances would be considered as common medals were it not for the addition of a particular bar or name. Such things are all too easy to produce for a collector who is not on guard against them.

It is no part of this book to go into the detail of such complexities. Many books by experts exist on the detail of particular battles, medals and forgeries. Here it is intended only to show the scope of the hobby, the methods of collecting and a broad picture useful to a beginner. The books necessary for a collector wishing to make a more advanced study of certain facets of the hobby are listed in Appendix II.

CHAPTER 1

ARMY MEDALS

THE true campaign medal, as it is awarded today, came into being as a result of the Battle of Waterloo and was first issued in 1815. In 1848 the Military General Service Medal was instituted by Queen Victoria and this was back-dated to cover battles as early as 1793.

But an enormous number of medals was issued privately, semi-officially and officially, before these awards. Bearing in mind that anyone can strike a medal and award it to whom he pleases, collectors need to find some rational reason for a medal's issue before they include it in their collection. Also, many medallions were struck to commemorate battles and these were sold to the general public as souvenirs. It is not always clear whether a medal was awarded or sold as a souvenir! There is still much research open to the new collector.

Before dealing with the true campaign medals we will mention some of the army medals which preceded them. The very first award to an individual for bravery is the famous Welch Medal. This gold medal with Charles I and Prince Charles on the obverse and the Royalist standard on the reverse was given to Sir Robert Welch who rescued a captured standard at the Battle of Edge Hill on October 23, 1642.

Apart from these, most awards were primarily for naval service and it was not until the award for the Capture and Defence of Gibraltar in 1704–05 that the army played a prominent role. Even then, the Royal Navy dominated the scene and Admiral Sir George Rooke received the surrender. But the army was there in force with the 1st and 2nd Foot Guards, and the 4th, 13th, 30th, 31st, 32nd and 35th Foot. Even so, only a few medals are known to have been awarded.

In 1746 the Culloden Medal was struck and experts still argue as to whether it is a true medal at all. It has been said that George II gave this award to senior officers who fought at the Battle of Culloden on April 16, 1746. But more probably it was struck entirely on behalf of the Cumberland Society for its members. At all events it is an interesting medal and marks an occasion in British history when the clan power was broken. The Duke of Cumberland who led British and Lowland Scottish forces was only about twenty-one at the time and the slaughter was vicious, even the wounded being bayoneted to death after the battle and the survivors hounded into the mountains.

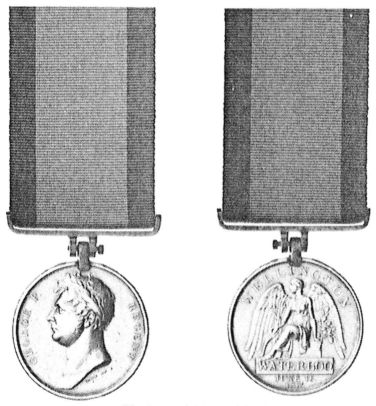

2. *The famous Waterloo Medal*

Another medal about which little is known is the Louisbourg Medal, showing a globe on the prostrate figure of France and the words 'Canada America'. A sailor and a soldier stand at the sides of the globe.

The inhabitants of St Vincent received a military award for the Carib War in 1773 to mark their part in crushing the native uprising. A few years later, in 1795, another medal was given for the Isle of St Vincent, this time to native soldiers who remained loyal to Britain when the French encouraged general revolt.

Colonel Musgrove presented medals to the 40th Foot during the American War of Independence when, on September 11, 1777, American forces made a night attack on German Town. Six companies of the 40th Foot held on to the storehouse building until relieved. The action was violent with nearly 2,000 dead and wounded.

It will be noted, however, that all these medals were awarded by individuals rather than by the British Crown and some interesting awards were made for the Defence of Gibraltar which took place between June 21, 1779 and February 2, 1783. General Picton had a medal produced showing Gibraltar and La Linea. The reverse bears the legend: 'By a zealous exertion of Patience perseverance and intrepidity after contending with an unparalleled succession of dangers and difficulties in the Defence of Gibraltar during a blockade and siege of almost four years, the Garrison under the auspices of George III triumphed over the combined powers of France and Spain'.

General Eliott also produced a medal for the Hanoverian troops which took part in the defence which also shows a view of Gibraltar. Other medals were struck, one of which is known as the Red Hot Shot Medal and shows a ship with fire-bombs hitting it. During the battle a red-hot shot set light to the *Talla Piedra*, one of ten battery ships designed by Jean Claude d'Arcon—and d'Arcon was serving on that ship. The batteries had been thought fire-proof, and as a result of the fire all ten battery ships were abandoned, much to the joy of the defenders.

A most unusual medal with a milled edge was presented to officers (in gold) and for non-commissioned officers and natives (in silver) by the Honourable East India Company for service in Gujerat 1778–84. Known as the Deccan Medal, it was the first of the medals by the Honourable East India Company which in themselves form a fascinating series and many collectors specialize in them. A Persian inscription is found on the Deccan Medal which translates: 'As coins are current in the world, so shall be the bravery and exploits of the heroes by whom the name of the victorious England nation was carried to the Deccan'.

A sepoy holding the Union Jack and the Flag of Mysore appears on the obverse of the Mysore Campaign Medal 1790–92. The medal was awarded by the British Government to native troops led by General Sir

3. *Military General Service Medal with bars for the Peninsular Campaign*

Ralph Abercromby and Maj.-Gen. Charles Cornwallis against Tippoo Sahib. There were two sizes of the medal: 1·7 inches and 1·5 inches in diameter. Varieties exist, as at the foot of the sepoy there are sometimes two cannon balls and sometimes more. A number of forgeries of this medal are known but these are invariably smaller in size.

The Seringapatam Medal was introduced to mark the eclipse of Tippoo Sahib, one of Britain's staunchest enemies, in 1799. Anticipating his plans to receive aid from Napoleon Bonaparte, Lord Mornington dispatched General Harris with 24,000 troops into Mysore and ordered another force of 7,000 under General Stuart to march from Bombay. A third force under the Nizam which included British troops joined them and on March 22, within two days' march of Seringapatam, the forces under Harris and the Nizam met Tippoo's army in a battle in which Colonel Wellesley (who became the Duke of Wellington) distinguished himself, and the success of the battle was credited to the 34th, his regiment.

On April 5 General Harris invested Seringapatam and though Tippoo made peace overtures they were not accepted. The city was carried by storm on May 4 and Tippoo was killed in the vicious hand-to-hand fighting. The medal shows the attack on the fortress by a scaling party on the reverse and the British Lion fighting a tiger on the obverse. Strangely, the medal had no means of suspension but recipients devised their own suspension rings.

The collector will have appreciated that most medals were introduced for senior officers in the first place and then gradually junior officers and men became eligible. However, in 1800 a medal of sorts was struck for the men only! Though not awarded for battle it went to marine soldiers as well as the sailors of the Ville de Paris and was the personal award of the Earl of St Vincent to his men who had not joined the 1797 mutiny. It is known as the Earl St Vincent's Medal.

The Egypt Medal of the Honourable East India Company was issued in 1801 to the forces under Major-General Sir David Baird and shows a sepoy with the Union Jack on the obverse and a ship and pyramids on the reverse. In 1850 a bar for this campaign was granted to the Military General Service Medal and it is to be noted that no soldier was eligible for both awards.

Behind every medal lies a story and all collectors would like to obtain one of the Highland Society's Medals awarded to the Black Watch (42nd Highlanders) by that society for the Highlanders' distinction on March 21, 1801. Napoleon's crack Invincible Legion lost its battle-standard to the Black Watch on that day. The engagement commenced as early as three o'clock in the morning while it was still dark. An attack was made on the British left, at Alexandria. It was a feint designed to draw the British to that quarter while a desperate charge was made on the British right, by the main strength of French cavalry. By ten o'clock in the morning the French were in full flight, leaving 1,700 men dead on the field of battle.

The medal shows on the obverse General Sir Ralph Abercromby who led the British and who was killed in the action. The reverse shows a Highlander and the date '21 MAR. 1801'. In the case of most awards only survivors were recipients, but on this occasion the High-land Society sent awards to the next of kin of those killed.

Many medals issued at this time are virtually unobtainable by ordinary collectors. For example, only thirteen gold medals were awarded for the battle at Maida on July 4, 1806, when a British force aided the King of Naples in his defeat of the French.

Sometimes the British soldier got no medal at all, while native forces in the same action did get medals. This happened with the Capture of Rodriguez, Isle of Bourbon and Isle of France which occurred between 1809 and 1810. The Honourable East India Company gave the award to native soldiers from Bombay and Bengal who took part. The reason why collectors much prefer to obtain medals awarded to British units rather than native troops is often because only a few were awarded to the British, as with the Java Medal of August 26, 1811. This was again issued by the Honourable East India Company; nearly 6,000 medals going to native troops and only 750 to Europeans. The medal depicts the attack on Fort Cornelis.

Military General Service Medal 1793-1814

On Easter Sunday, April 10, 1814, Wellington's troops, tired from crossing the Garonne rapids the day before, fell on the French batteries at Toulouse. Numerically even, the French enjoyed well fortified heights, bristling with cannon, and a network of vineyards and orchards surrounded by stone walls as a natural protection. They were successfully dislodged and on the 12th the Duke of Wellington rode into Toulouse as victor. Little did the soldiers realize then that thirty-four years later a medal would be given to them for that battle. This was the Military General Service Medal authorized by General Order of June 1, 1847 and it encompassed battles from 1793 to the action at Toulouse in 1814. To qualify, a soldier had to have stayed alive as well as fought in the action! The medal was not awarded to next of kin and it follows that a large number of men who fought at the turn of the century were no longer able to claim the award in 1848. In all, twenty-nine bars were issued—a bar for each battle and some soldiers were able to claim a good number of the bars.

Two men were entitled to fifteen of the twenty-nine bars and the medal roll shows that nine men earned fourteen. Such medals are, of

21

course, priceless. The collector has to be very careful when buying medals with several bars. It is not unknown for forgers to obtain genuine medals and genuine bars in order to make up one medal with a good number of bars giving it a 'great rarity'. The collector will find everything genuine with such a forgery and his only recourse is to study the medal rolls to establish that the recipient was entitled to the bars that appear on the medal.

Nor is this always an infallible test. Applications for medal bars were not always granted and it is known that an applicant could be given bars for which he had not applied and which were not on the medal roll. Faced with a medal of this sort the new collector is well advised to take it to one of the larger medal dealers before paying out a large sum of money for it.

Most collectors, however, are happy enough to get this medal with one or two bars. Approximately 25,000 medals were awarded. It is a good medal for a specialist to concentrate on as it covers the Peninsular War (21 bars) as well as other major conflicts. They were:

Egypt	1801	Java	1811
Maida	1806	Ciudad Rodrigo	1812
Roleia	1808	Badajoz	1812
Vimiera	1808	Salamanca	1812
Sahagun	1808	Fort Detroit	1813
Sahagun and		Vittoria	1813
Benevente	1808/9	Pyrenees	1813
Benevente	1809	St Sebastian	1813
Corunna	1809	Chateauguay	1813
Martinique	1809	Nivelle	1813
Talavera	1809	Chrystler's	
Guadalupe	1810	Farm	1813
Busaco	1810	Nive	1813
Barrosa	1811	Orthes	1814
Fuentes d'Onor	1811	Toulouse	1814
Albuhera	1811		

The medal shows the head of Queen Victoria on the obverse with the words VICTORIA REGINA and the date 1848. The reverse design shows the Queen placing a laurel wreath on the victor who is kneeling. The words 'To the British Army' and the dates '1793–1814'.

Bars were authorized on different dates and the earliest award, that of Egypt 1801, was not authorized until 1850. Whether or not it was intended to issue bars for actions in 1793 is not known but the date is misleading in so far as no bars were issued for events earlier than 1801.

Although good advice to the beginner is that if a medal has been doctored in any way be very wary about it—the fact remains that some of the Military General Service Medals will be found with renaming of the 'rank'. This is because an officer on promotion would bring his medal up to date with his rank.

There are many ways in which this medal is collected by specialists. The obvious way is to obtain one of each bar—though some of these are hard to find. The Benevente bar was only awarded to ten soldiers; 7th Light Dragoons (4), 10th Light Dragoons (4), 18th Light Dragoons (1) and Royal Artillery (1). Another method is to collect the medals of a Line Regiment, one for each action the regiment was represented at. The 95th for example was present at twenty of the twenty-nine battles commemorated with bars. The 42nd was at sixteen. A good number of line regiments fought at ten or more of the engagements. The Royal Artillery is probably the only branch of the army which was present at all twenty-nine.

A collection of the Peninsular bars is the easiest as most of them had well over a thousand claimants (Roleia and Barrosa were the only two with less than a thousand).

Another interesting way of collecting these medals is by the different theatre of war bars. Egypt, Maida, America, West Indies, Peninsular, Java, Martinque, etc. It is possible to find medals with different theatre of war combinations.

Most of these are difficult to come by but the most often met with is the Peninsular and Egypt combination. Medals exist with bars for three different theatres of war such as Egypt, Maida and Peninsular.

If the men who fought at Toulouse in 1814 had to wait many years to get their awards, the soldiers who fought in Nepal were luckier.

CHAPTER 2

NAVAL MEDALS

THROUGHOUT much of the history of the British Isles, sea power has been the major factor in preventing foreign invasion. Well aware of the importance of this, the nation developed its naval forces to a pitch where the power was such that at one time any ship in the Channel was obliged to dip its colours to a British man-of-war as it passed.

The first British medals of which we have any knowledge are those awarded to men of its navy. The 'Ark in Flood' medal of Elizabeth I was given to Admirals and Commanders who fought against the Armada on July 29, 1588. They were awarded in gold and silver and had rings and chains attached to them so that the medal could be worn around the neck. Our knowledge of this period is not complete and several variations of Elizabeth I medals exist. Even more exquisite than the 'Ark in Flood' is the 'Bay Tree Medal' which gets its name from the bay tree shown on the reverse.

There are also individual medals such as Drake's Medal, a personal award to Sir Francis Drake from Elizabeth I. This award is set with diamonds and rubies and consists of a cameo cut in onyx, attributed to Vincenteno. The reverse contains a miniature of Elizabeth by Nicholas Hilliard, with the date 1575.

Awards by Charles I were sometimes so large that it is doubtful if they were intended as medals to be worn so much as commemorative pieces. One of these was the medal issued for the launching of the *Royal Sovereign* which took place in 1637. Again a number of varieties exist.

It will be seen that the practice of giving medal awards for war service started with the Navy. So did the practice of making awards to men of all ranks. The Commonwealth Naval Medal was issued in 1649 to both officers and men for having 'done good service at sea'. Designed by one of the greatest British engravers of all time, Thomas

Simon, it depicts Parliament in session and, on the reverse, cartouches of St George's Cross and the Harp, and an anchor on whose stock can be found the initials of Thomas Simon. Simon had to give a surety of £500 that he would 'make no unlawful use of the presse' while striking these medals in the Tower of London.

During the night of July 31, 1650, the 22-gun *Adventure* commanded by Robert Wyard, gave battle to six Royalist frigates and the conflict continued throughout the next day until the Royalist forces withdrew. For this the Wyard Medal was awarded in gold and silver and has the inscription: 'Service–don–against–six–ships etc'. An oval medal, it is 1·6 inches by 1·35 inches.

From records of Parliament we can sometimes get full details of awards such as those for the Dutch Wars, which produced some of the most attractive British navy medals. A major engagement which took place in 1653 saw the utter defeat of Admiral Van Tromp and Admiral De Ruyter. This was a memorable occasion for the Army too as it was the first battle in which soldiers served at sea and it gave rise to the Royal Marines. The Dutch lost 26 ships to Britain's two and Parliament voted to award Generals Blake and Monk gold chains. Chains of lesser value were awarded to Vice-Admiral Penn and Rear-Admiral Lawson and smaller chains to the selected staff officers. The remainder of £2,000 designated for awards was spent on medals for officers of the fleet. Four different types were issued.

Charles II legitimized the distribution of prize money by a proclamation in 1665 in which he also decided that a portion of prize money should be given to the widows of the men who were killed in an action which resulted in prize money.

The Dutch War of 1665 has left several varieties of medal for collectors; some by Thomas Rawlins and Roettier, both famous engravers. The Roettier medal, two inches in diameter, has the motto 'PRO TALIBVS AVSIS' (for such enterprises). It is not always possible to decide whether a medal was commemorative or for decoration and some of these, being undated, could have been awarded for either the first or second Dutch Wars—or both. Although the war ended in 1667 it flared up again in 1672.

Queen Mary distributed some £30,000 to soldiers and sailors following the battle of La Hogue in 1692, which secured her position. At the same time she commissioned gold medals and silver medals for officers.

The reverse side shows the French Admiral's flagship *Le Soleil Royal* burning.

William and Mary continued to award special medals for individual service at sea and did not differentiate between fighting-forces and civilians. Medals were on occasion given to fishermen who engaged privateers of the enemy.

With the victory at Vigo during the reign of Queen Anne, Britain had enough captured bullion to mark its coinage with the word 'Vigo' to show where the silver came from. The Queen had medals struck for the chief officers.

Individual medals were struck, such as one to Captain James Lamprière (a gold medal): 'for his Zeal to her Service, and his Successful Conducting ye Squadron commanded by Rear-Admiral Dilkes, who destroyed a considerable number of ye enemy's Merchant Ships under convoy of 3 Men of War on their own coast'.

Lamprière was also to receive the Granville award of 1703 following a naval victory off Granville in Normandy in July of that year. While no official record exists for these, it is believed they were struck by order of the Queen for the Rear-Admiral and his officers.

At this time we have the first reference to an award to a boy for gallantry. Queen Anne presented such medals 'to give all due Encouragement to the Valour and Fidelity of Her Subjects serving aboard any of Her Majesties Ships of War or Privateers', and the cost of the awards came from her personal share of the prize monies. The award to a boy has a reverse inscription: 'Her Majesties reward to Robert Taylor Boy of Ye Mary Galley, for his Zeal and Courage at ye taking of ye French Privateer Jacques La Blonde of Dunkirk'.

Medals were issued during the reigns of George I and II, though often these were more of a commemorative nature than battle awards. A number of Vernon medals (named after Admiral Edward Vernon) exist in different sizes and made of silver, bronze and white metal with the inscription: 'He took Porto Bello with Six Ships only', but it is doubtful if they were official decorations. Medals struck by T. Pingo in gold, silver and bronze were made following the victory at Louisbourg in 1758.

A decisive sea victory during the reign of King George III led to awards for the Glorious First of June, 1794. Admiral Lord Howe destroyed the French fleet off Ushant, and the King instituted medals for the occasion. The King and Queen boarded the Admiral's flagship on his return and made presentation of jewelled swords and at the same time announced that a special medal would be struck for principal officers.

This was the Naval Gold Medal awarded in 1796. There were two types. The larger one was worn round the neck by Admirals and the smaller medal for flag officers was pinned to the uniform through a button-hole by the white ribbon with dark blue edges (which was to become the ribbon for the Naval General Service Medal in 1847).

The Naval Gold Medal was awarded for actions up until 1815 but mostly went to ranks of post captain and above. Only 140 were issued, and of these only two went to lower ranks, Lieutenant Pinfold (HMS *Ajax*) and Lieutenant Stockham (HMS *Thunderer*). Both officers commanded their ships in the absence of the captains at Trafalgar but even so were not given the awards until they had been promoted to post captains.

These and previous awards are, generally speaking, of such rarity that new collectors are unlikely to come across them. Only a selection of them has been mentioned to give an idea of the sort of awards that were made and the historic importance attached to them.

With the advent of Lord Nelson, Britain's most famous sailor, sea medals were to become not merely the prerogative of senior naval officers. Following the battle of the Nile, Nelson's prize agent, Alexander Davison, gave medals to all who had participated. Gold medals went to the captains, silver to warrant officers, bronze-gilt to petty officers and bronze to seamen. Designed by C. H. Kuchler it is the first known award made by a private person which was accepted for official wearing.

The Naval Gold Medal, first awarded for the Glorious First of June, was distributed to senior officers at Trafalgar (in fact the award was given for eighteen different naval actions, the final occasion being the battle between the *Endymion* and the American *President* on January 15, 1815).

For some reason the poor ordinary seaman was still ignored by official awards and after Trafalgar a private citizen decided to follow in the footsteps of Nelson's agent by issuing a medal to all who took part in the famous battle. He was Matthew Boulton, partner of James Watt of the Soho Mint at Birmingham. The obverse of the medal, struck in silver for officers and in pewter for the lower deck, shows Lord Nelson.

Unlike the Nile awards, however, the seamen did not seem to appreciate the Trafalgar award. Pewter was common, but the intrinsic value was useless to a seaman, so many of the pewter medals were flung overboard.

Nelson's agent also issued a medal known as Davison's Trafalgar Medal. It has been said that this was for the crew of HMS *Victory*, Nelson's flagship. Some of these were also struck in pewter, or white metal.

4. *Naval Long Service and Good Conduct Medal*

Nonetheless, the seamen who gave Britain its greatest sea victory were destined to receive an official medal. They had to wait a long time for it, however, as it was left to Queen Victoria to issue a General Order in 1847 announcing a medal for naval engagements from 1793 to 1815. The time was later extended to 1840 and the first distribution of the award was made in January 1849. It was only awarded to men who had survived the actions and were alive at the time of the award. Two hundred and thirty bars were authorized for the medal and a total of 20,900 claims was made. It is one of the most popular items among collectors, and specialists attempt to get as many bars as they can. Some of the bars were awarded in such small numbers that it would, today, be impossible to complete such a collection. Indeed, only a few of the larger actions are available at reasonable prices.

Whereas it is not always possible to determine the exact number of bars, the table given in Appendix I (p. 97) is a good guide to the rarity of such bars. Where none has been issued the bar was authorized, but not claimed. This could easily occur if the seamen entitled to it were killed in subsequent action.

With 230 different bars the issue of the Naval General Service Medal covers the period of history when Britain's supremacy at sea was vital.

5. *Naval General Service Medal with bar*

As well as the bars listed there were 56 bars awarded for Boat Service. These were occasions where ship's boats were launched for action, sometimes in large numbers. But often a single ship's boat would engage the enemy with such distinction that a bar was awarded. Such bars have inscriptions giving the date and month, then the words 'Boat Service' followed by the year. For example: '1st May Boat Service 1810'—a bar awarded to eighteen men who took part in a landing from HMS *Nereide* at Jacotel, Bay of Biscay. Over 100 sailors attacked and destroyed the shore battery and then captured a French merchant vessel to make their getaway.

To own one of these is to own a bit of history. Unfortunately most of them are very expensive. Today few boat service medals can be obtained for less than £80 and many of the general bars are just as expensive. In fact only Algiers, Navarino and Syria could be considered reasonably available at prices between £14 and £25. The Trafalgar bar fetches around £70.

But for those able to meet such prices the fascination of the Naval General Service Medal is obvious. Even with the three relatively common bars, interesting—and difficult to form—collections can be made. The battle of Algiers fought on August 27, 1816, was for the suppression of piracy and slavery. The Algerians had accumulated several thousand Christian slaves and Lord Exmouth was sent with five ships of the line and eight smaller fighting ships to seek their release. He was joined by six Dutch frigates at Gibraltar and the combined fleets bombarded the city until the Dey accepted the terms imposed. Some 1,200 Christians were released immediately. The Algerians were to cause more trouble later and in 1830 the French colonized the territory. A special medal—the Exmouth Gold Medal—was struck for Lord Exmouth with an exergue inscription: 'Algiers Bombarded Its Fleet Destroyed and Christian Slavery Extinguished, August 27, 1816.' Ships taking part were: *Queen Charlotte, Albion, Granicus, Glasgow, Hebrus, Impregnable, Leander, Minden, Prometheus, Severn, Superb, Britomart, Cordelia, Heron, Jasper, Mutine, Beelzebub, Fury, Hecla,* and *Infernal*, apart from transport vessels. A medal from each ship would be hard to find but worth the attempt.

Equally interesting is the battle of Navarino, for which a similarly large number of medals was issued. Following a revolt by the Greeks, the Turks began a ruthless suppression which shook the world when the inhabitants of Morea were slaughtered *en masse*. French, Russian and British warships moved into the harbour at Navarino, requiring the Pasha to cease such reprisals against the Greeks. A Turkish ship fired on a British longboat killing the officer commanding it. Within moments HMS *Dartmouth* fired a full broadside and the great sea-battle was on. The Allied fleets lost fewer than 200 men, their enemies having thousands killed.

In order to maintain Britain's dominance it was important that the balance of power should not change too much and when Mohammed Ali, Pasha of Egypt, defeated the Turks and made himself master of

30

Syria in 1839, Britain thought it was time to act. The Pasha would not observe an ultimatum that Syria was to be restored to the Sultan of Turkey and, without further ado, Britain's warships, supported by other nations, blockaded Alexandria where the Egyptian fleet was at anchor. A number of engagements were fought, the more notable being Beirut, Tyre, Sidon and Acre, before the Pasha conceded. With over 7,000 bars issued for this event, the collector has a better chance of forming a representative collection of this bar. Thirty-four British warships took part.

Very difficult to find are the medals awarded to soldiers who took part in the actions entitling them to the Syria bar (72 were awarded), and most men who earned the Syria bar were also given a special award by the Sultan of Turkey. This is known as the St Jean d'Acre Medal 1840. It shows the Turkish flag flying on the Fortress of Acre, captured for him by the British.

No less interesting but much easier to find are the medals awarded to the navy for the China War of 1842 which currently fetch around £18 each. A large number of warships took part and the specialist soon learns which are the scarce ships to look for. This is where specialization pays dividends. The general collector or dealer cannot hope to learn such details about all medals so it is still possible for those who have taken the trouble to learn all about the event to pick up a rare medal.

A good example of this is the Punjab Campaign Medal 1848-9 for which three bars were issued—Mooltan, Chilianwala and Goojerat. It is common enough to Indian troops and sells for about £15 when awarded to most of the line regiments taking part. But this medal was also awarded to seamen and is rare in such cases. One hundred seamen under Commander F. T. Powell were at the siege of Mooltan—the first occasion seamen were engaged in battle so far from their warships.

Medals were also issued for the Second China War 1857–60 and were issued unnamed to the Royal Navy though many seamen had their names inscribed on them. Five different bars were issued to this medal and a genuine medal with all the bars is extremely rare.

The Scinde Medal 1843 was also issued to the navy and the Indian General Service Medal can be found with the bar 'Pegu' to men of the Royal Navy who had eight ships in the action together with the East India Company's 22 vessels.

The Navy played a substantial part in the Crimea War, for which a special medal with five bars was issued, one of them—Azoff—entirely for naval action. It is impossible for anyone to have earned all five bars for that reason. But some of the marines serving ashore were able to get the four bars which could be obtained by some regiments, and the Naval Brigade were, in some cases, awarded three bars.

Every year at the Royal Tournament the public can see the Royal Navy 'run the guns', taking field-guns over an imaginary ravine, assemble them and fire all in a matter of minutes. Teams from the Navy compete with each other for speed. In the days of the Crimean War the Naval Brigade were doing this in earnest and at Sebastopol more than a thousand seamen landed with 50 heavy guns where, at speed, they prepared for battle—to the embarrassment of the artillery units whose preparations took longer.

The Crimea Medal is a good choice for a new collector who wishes to have a fairly large number of medals available, a number of different ships involved, and not too much expense. A lot has been written about the Crimea and it is not difficult to research—though the specialist can always find avenues for research which are unusual.

Forty-three warships took part in the blockade of the Baltic for which the Baltic Medal 1854–55 was issued. During this time the Navy blockaded and subsequently captured the port of Bomarsund; Sveaborg was also attacked.

Sailors also took part in the Indian Mutiny for which a medal was issued (1857–58). Indeed, awards to men of the brigades from HMS *Pearl* and *Shannon* are among the most desirable. A brigade of 250 men from *Pearl* fought in twenty battles during the Indian Mutiny. A larger force from *Shannon* was present at some of the major engagements. In one engagement four VCs were awarded to naval personnel.

The Persia, 1857 bar; the two New Zealand Medals (1845–47 and 1860–66 for Maori uprisings); Abyssinia; Ashantee; Perak bar and South Africa Medal 1877–79 can all be found named to men of the Royal Navy. Particularly sought after are those of the small brigade from HMS *Active* who took part in the Zulu War in 1879, being attached to Captain Campbell's third column.

The Egypt Medal (1882–89) can be collected with different bars —thirteen were awarded, and a number of them were awarded to seamen. Of particular interest to specialists in Navy medals are those

6. *A specialized collection of the Crimean War Medal—one to each warship taking part in the first Fleet attack at Sebastopol. Top right are the Turkish Crimean Medals*

with the bar Tel-el-Kebir. Lieutenant Wyatt Rawson, RN, navigated the Highland Brigade over the desert to Tel-el-Kebir by plotting the stars (he was killed in the action which followed) and both marines and naval brigade took part. The marines had large casualties, forming the front line of General Graham's brigade.

The El-Teb-Tamaai bar to a seaman shows that he fought side by

33

side with the Black Watch. It was naval machine-guns which stopped the headlong rush of the fanatical Mahdists.

The Abu-Klea bar was also awarded to seamen—eight were killed in the action. A naval gun was positioned on the left flank of the formed square, and at the critical time, jammed. Its crew fell to the spears of the Mahdists with the exception of Lord Charles Beresford who commanded the naval brigade and had taken charge of the gun himself. Knocked out by the feed-plate which he had been unscrewing to free the blockage, he survived to tell the story: ". . . they were tearing down on us with a roar like the roar of the sea, an immense, surging wave of white-sashed black forms brandishing bright spears and long flashing swords and chanting, as they leaped and ran, the war song of their faith . . ." Few Arabs penetrated the square, however, and all of them died for their trouble.

The East and West Africa Medal 1887–1900 went to the Royal Navy, in some cases a total of 14 different bars out of 23 being awarded to seamen. For the most part these were naval brigades, often proceeding up river in small numbers and taking on war canoes and spears in punitive expeditions. It is sometimes possible to learn details about individual men who took part in these battles. The medal collector sometimes finds the philatelic auctions a happy hunting ground—for occasionally mail sent home by such fighting men comes up for auction at very reasonable prices. To find a letter from a man whose medal has already been acquired adds great interest to the collection.

The Boer War was fought on a massive scale—though the ratio of British to Boers was grossly unequal and could only lead to the defeat of the Boers. However, it took longer than it was thought it would, and medals had to have the dates 'rubbed out' (they can still be seen) to cater for a longer war. The Royal Navy took its share of the war which resulted in 26 different bars being issued. Medals with bars to the navy are quite rare but a number can be found, as for the Defence of Ladysmith to men of HMS *Powerful*, and Relief of Ladysmith to men of HMS *Terrible* and *Philomel*. The rare bar 'Wepener' is known to have been awarded to sailors.

The Africa General Service Medal was awarded to the Navy with bars for their parts in Jubaland, Gambia 1901, Aro 1901–02, Somaliland 1902–04, and Somaliland 1908–10.

An unusual award to seamen was the Transport Medal. This award

34

was made on the instructions of King Edward VII who had been impressed with the efficiency of the transport system in the South Africa and China campaigns. It went to hospital ships and transports.

Those whose sphere of interest is the Royal Navy will find no shortage of campaigns and battles. Even a general naval collection of one of each major campaign would take some getting together today, and a collection would take on large proportions if each different bar entitled to the navy was added. Specialist collections are made of major wars or battles, of awards to naval brigades and so on. Collections can be enhanced with pictures of warships from which medals in the collection belong. A number of famous British ships have borne the same name down through the years and a highly specialized collection could be made of certain ships, covering over a hundred years.

CHAPTER 3

THE BATTLE OF WATERLOO

THE Waterloo Medal of 1815 is the best starting-point for new collectors who set out to compile a collection of the campaign medals of the British Army.

This medal is the first to be awarded to all personnel present at a battle (the Dunbar Medal had been given to officers and men but not to *all* taking part).

It was the first campaign medal to have the recipient's name impressed on the edge by machine and it was also the first campaign medal to be given to next of kin. (The Highland Society Medal was not a Government Campaign Medal but a private one.) The new collector might be confused on being told that the Waterloo Medal was the first Government medal to all troops when he comes up against a Military General Service Medal with a bar for an earlier battle—but the Military General Service Medal was not awarded until 1848 and was back-dated to 1793 but even then only awarded to survivors. (See medal illustrations on pages 17 and 19).

Experts argue the toss about many earlier 'campaign' medals, and often contend that such-and-such was a commemoration medallion rather than a battle award, etc. There is no doubt about the Waterloo Medal and it is therefore an excellent starting-point. The collector can always work backwards later on once he has gained the knowledge necessary to form his own opinions of the experts' assessments on earlier awards.

Also, of course, few battles can match Waterloo for importance in modern British history. Waterloo was a turning point; it established the supremacy of the British at a time when the domination of Europe was very much a matter of the toss of a coin.

The collector must expect these medals to be fairly expensive, but they are by no means out of reach. Generally they can be obtained from about £30. General Colville's reserve division which was not committed to battle naturally gave rise to the cheaper medals. This division comprised: 2/35th, 1/54th, 2/59th and 1/91st Foot.

A little-appreciated fact is that the Waterloo Medal was awarded for other battles, namely the battle of Ligny and the battle of Quatre Bras, both of which took place on June 16, two days before the main conflict at Waterloo.

Because the medal was awarded very soon after the action (early in 1816) it was worn on the breast and suffered the wear and tear of a soldier's life, so that these medals seldom turn up in condition better than Very Fine and more often are only found in Fine condition.

Whereas collectors become very sceptical about 'unofficial' suspenders, etc. on other medals, private forms of suspension on the Waterloo Medal do not adversely affect the value of the medal. When issued it had what is probably the most ugly form of suspension of any British award—a heavy steel ring which quickly became rusty, and marked the resplendent uniforms of the wearers. Officers in particular soon took the ring off and replaced it with a more attractive and less cumbersome form of suspension.

Fifty thousand-odd fought under the Duke of Wellington, while Napoleon, who discounted Blücher's ability to rally his forces for a further three days, moved to his battle positions with 75,000 men, full of confidence. Looking at a scant patrol of British troops, Napoleon is supposed to have said: "I have them there at last, these English!" General Foy, who had ample experience of 'these English' in Spain, retorted: "Wellington never shows his troops; but if he be yonder, I must warn your majesty that the English infantry, in close fighting, is the very devil!"

And so they were. The price they paid for victory was terrible— fifteen thousand dead and wounded. Some regiments were virtually wiped out and after the battle the Duke of Wellington rode the field able to trace the 'squares', marked clearly by the dead. At the time the Duke wrote: "The losses I have sustained have quite broken me down, and I have no feeling for the advantages we have gained". But it was the salvation of British interests and the end of the Grande Armée.

Small wonder that the medal of this battle is highly prized and marks the starting-point of many collections. Each medal is named to its owner on the edge in machine-impressed serif letters. The machine was the invention of Thomas Jerome and Charles Harrison, who were employed at the Mint. Where the new collector comes across such a medal with an engraved name it means that the medal has been re-named. It is then of little real value.

Although no forgeries of the medal are known there was a replacement medal produced and new collectors should be careful not to buy one as an original. They are easy to distinguish as, apart from being smaller in size, the name of the designer, T. Wyon, is omitted from the replacement on both obverse and reverse. Sometimes bars are met with. These are not official, but may well have been produced contemporarily as an added embellishment to the medal when being worn in civilian clothes.

CHAPTER 4

AFRICA

THE vastness of Africa becomes apparent to the collector of war medals issued for service on that Continent. These recall the exploits of British soldiers fighting under all kinds of conditions from the dark African forests to the sun-baked sands. Africa is a continent which, from a military point of view, has encompassed every type of warfare—from repelling small bands of warriors armed with spears to Boer commando tactics and the tank tactics of Rommel.

Because some of the battles in the early days were small—sometimes little more than skirmishes—the collector can enjoy himself searching through little-read accounts of these activities with a good chance of coming across the actual name of a man which perhaps adorns the edge of a medal in his possession.

The large number of medals relating to Africa testify to the continuous troubles in this part of the once-mighty British Empire. Ashanti is a part of Western Africa in the interior of the former Gold Coast. Several awards were made to the British soldiers for warfare in this territory.

Ashanti first came into the news in 1807 when King Sy Tutu attacked a British fort on the coast. In 1824 following more attacks the Governor of Cape Coast Castle, Sir Charles MacCarthy, advanced with a small force only to be wiped out at Esmacow. He was avenged at the battle of Dudowah in 1826. Again, in 1863, war broke out when Governor Pine refused to hand over some runaway slaves to the Ashanti King. Against this background we come to King 'Coffee' Calcali, who renewed the war with success until he met Colonel Festing, and later Sir Garnet Wolseley with British troops.

For this war the Ashanti War Medal was struck covering the period 1873–74. After the recipient's name on the edge, there is either the date 1873–4 or '73–'74. Many of the recipients also qualified for the East and West Africa Medal, which was exactly the same as the Ashanti War Medal except that it was slightly thinner, having the diademed head of Victoria on the obverse and a battle scene on the reverse.

Although servicemen were only supposed to receive one or the other, in fact examples are known where men were in possession of both medals. The Ashanti Medal had one bar for Coomassie. This was the capital of King 'Coffee' and English troops under Sir Garnet Wolseley entered the capital on February 5, 1874 and fired it. During the march back envoys of the Ashanti King arrived and sued for peace, agreeing to pay 50,000 ounces of gold.

In 1896 there was more trouble and the Ashanti Star was struck and issued unnamed to forces taking part. It was a bronze star and particularly prized are those of the 2nd battalion West Yorkshire Regiment, whose colonel had them all named at his own expense.

The fierce Ashanti continued to give trouble and war broke out in 1900. It did not last long and marked the end of Ashanti problems. A medal was struck showing King Edward VII on the obverse and the British lion on a rock above a native shield and assegais and the word 'Ashanti'. One bar was issued for Kumassi which was besieged by the Ashanti. The war lasted from March 31 to December 25, 1900.

Few more difficult campaigns have ever been undertaken. The advance occurred in the unhealthy rainy season against 40,000 Ashanti using the dense forests as protection.

Another part of Africa, the Sudan, has been the scene of fierce conflicts between the British and the inhabitants, and different medals have been issued to mark the events with many bars. It is a good area for the specialist and a collection of the various bars can show the progress of the war in the Sudan.

The Anglo-Egyptian Sudan covered one million square miles and embraced a multitude of different tribes from the Bejas ('The Fuzzies') to the Berbers and the Baggara—the fierce horsemen who provided the Khalifa with his fanatical bodyguard.

No better description of the Sudan at that time was ever given than that by a famous war correspondent at the Battle of Omdurman: 'The Sudan is a depopulated desert. Northwards of Khartoum it is a wilderness—southwards a devastation. It was always a poor country and always must be. Slaves and ivory were its wealth in old time, but now ivory is all but exterminated and slaves must be sold no more. It has no colour and no age; just a monotone of squalid barbarism. Its people are naked and dirty, ignorant and besotted. It is a quarter of a continent of sheer squalor. The Sudan is a God accursed wilderness, an empty limbo of torment for ever and ever.'

The Queen's Sudan Medal 1896–97 embraced the famous battle of Omdurman. This was probably the last of the 'old world' type of battles where the British formed up two deep with their backs to the Nile. As the Dervish hordes attacked, the front rank of the line fired until the rifles were too hot to hold and the men had to change rifles with the back row. A correspondent wrote: "The storm was met with a concentrated fire from all arms of our left wing; before its withering blast the followers of the Prophet fell like the ripe wheat in fertile Himalayan valleys, threshed by a hailstorm."

"The final effort of the fighting members of the Khalifa's own family or clan were heroic. Spurning the devastating cross-fire they carried their hundreds of white flags, like the actual crest of a toppling wave, against Hector Macdonald's Sudanese, gathering an impetus which hurled them on, on, on even in death, until but a trickle of panting humanity rolled up to the line of scientific weapons. There the Black Banner of the Khalifa was planted in the sand, and it may truly be said that round that banner Mahdism died."

The 21st Lancers particularly distinguished themselves when, while making a charge, they found themselves confronted by the Khalifa's reserves hidden in an entrenched ravine. Being committed, they charged on into a blaze of fire that came from a foe twenty deep, and hacked and hewed their way through the living mass.

The medals which were issued in both silver and bronze currently fetch around £7 for silver and £18 for bronze. The medal had no bars.

The award was not made until 1899 and was given to all those who took part in the reconquest of the Sudan. The reverse shows Victory seated with trophy and flags and the word 'Sudan'. The ribbon is black, yellow and scarlet, said to represent the Dervish army (black), the desert (yellow) and the thin red line of British (scarlet).

The Khedive of Egypt also made a medal award—the Khedive's Sudan Medal in 1897. Although this covered the same period it was used also for subsequent campaigns up until 1905. In all fifteen bars were issued (they are in English and Arabic):

Firket (June 7, 1896)
Hafir (September 19–26, 1896)
Abu Hamed (July 7, 1897)
Sudan 1897
The Atbara (April 8, 1898)
Khartoum (September 2, 1898)
Gedaref (September 7 to December 26, 1898)
Gedid (November 22, 1899)
Sudan 1899
Bahr-el-Ghazal 1900–02
Jerok (January to March, 1904)
Nyam-Nyam (January to May, 1905)
Talodi (June 2–15, 1905)
Katfia (April 1908)
Nyima (November 1–21, 1908)

Some of these medals are known with as many as ten bars, but they were seldom awarded to British troops with more than two bars. The rarest of these, when awarded singly, is the bar for the Atbara. This battle was fought on a Good Friday, the Anglo-Egyptian army reaching its objective at six o'clock in the morning. At a quarter to eight the infantry stormed the zariba. The enemy behaved with their accustomed bravery, but their fire was too high to check the stormers. The Cameron Highlanders and the 11th Sudanese suffered the most but the victory was complete.

The next Sudan Campaign medal was the Sudan Medal of 1910. The reverse shows a lion on a plinth and the word 'Sudan'. This medal had sixteen bars, and these are rarer, in most cases, than those of the earlier medal.

Atwot (February to April, 1910)
S. Kordofan (November 10 to December 19, 1910)
Sudan 1912
Zeraf 1913–14
Mandal (March 1914)
Miri (April 1915)
Mongalla 1915–16
Darfur 1916
Fasher (September 1 to November 23, 1916)

42

Lau Nuer (March to May, 1917)
Nyima 1917–18
Atwot 1918
Garjak Nuer (December 1919 to April 1920)
Aliab Dinka (November 8, 1919 to May 1920)
Nyala (December 26, 1921 to January 20, 1922)
Darfur 1921.

In 1918 the medal was altered to carry the cypher of the new
Khedive and a new Arabic date. These medals, issued in bronze and
silver, were unnamed. (The bronze medals were without bars.)

Warrior natives of South Africa who really caused trouble by their
prowess were the Zulus and the Kaffirs. The South Africa Campaign
Medal 1834–53 was issued for wars against the Kaffirs in 1834–35,

7. *South Africa Medal, 1834–53*

1846–47, and 1850–53 and the South Africa Medal for the Zulu and
Basuto Wars of 1877–79. This last medal had the same design as the
South Africa Campaign Medal but the date was omitted and replaced
with crossed assegais and a Zulu shield. Six bars were awarded but only
one to each medal. The bars had the dates:

1877, 1877–8, 1878, 1878–9, 1877–8–9, 1879.

The last occasion on which there was a truly mighty uprising against
British rule by the Zulus—whose giant warriors were organized into

8. *A display of medals awarded for the Zulu War to members of the Naval Brigade. Only a few hundred men were engaged and these medals are all very rare*

regiments wearing different coloured feathers round the calves for identification—occurred in 1906. The rebellion was ruthlessly suppressed and a silver medal, Natal 1906, was granted by the Natal Government in 1908 to those taking part. The obverse shows the head of King Edward VII and the reverse a female figure holding the sword of justice and a palm. She stands on a pile of captured native weapons and is supported by Britannia holding the Orb of the Empire. The naming on this medal is usually by means of impressed thin square capitals and is often quite hard to see.

But Britain was to have more or less continuous trouble in Africa and the Africa General Service Medal 1902 was issued to encompass military operations from 1901 and lasted until the death of King Edward VII when the obverse was changed to the bust of King George V. This was done in 1916.

A large number of bars was issued:

N. Nigeria	East Africa 1915
N. Nigeria 1902	East Africa 1918
N. Nigeria 1903	West Africa 1906
N. Nigeria 1903/4	West Africa 1908
N. Nigeria 1904	West Africa 1909/10
N. Nigeria 1906	Somaliland 1901
S. Nigeria	Somaliland 1902/4
S. Nigeria 1902	Somaliland 1908/10
S. Nigeria 1902/3	Somaliland 1920
S. Nigeria 1903	Jidballi
S. Nigeria 1903/4	Uganda 1900
S. Nigeria 1904	B.C.A. 1899–1900
S. Nigeria 1904/5	Jubaland
S. Nigeria 1905	Jubaland 1917/18
S. Nigeria 1905/6	Gambia
Nigeria 1918	Aro 1901/02
East Africa 1902	Lango 1901
East Africa 1904	Kissi 1905
East Africa 1905	Nandi 1905/06
East Africa 1906	Shimber Berris 1914/15
East Africa 1913	Nyasaland 1915
East Africa 1914	Kenya
East Africa 1913/14	

Another part of Africa where British troops were called upon to fight was Abyssinia and the Abyssinian War Medal was awarded for operations between October 1867 and April 1868.

The obverse has a veiled bust of Queen Victoria in a nine-pointed star design. The name of the recipient appeared on the reverse inside the laurel wreath. The war was concluded with the capture of Magdala.

Egypt, the scene of fierce Napoleonic warfare necessitated military actions again in 1882 and the Egypt Medal 1882–1889 was awarded with thirteen bars:

Alexandria 11th July	The Nile 1884–85
Tel-el-Kebir	Abu Klea
El-Teb	Kirbekan
Tamaai	Suakin 1885
El-Teb-Tamaai	Gemaizah
Suakin 1884	Toski

At the same time the Khedive's Egyptian Stars were issued for the period 1882–91. There were four issues: 1882; 1884; 1884–86 and an undated star. A bar was issued for Tokar.

There are many other medals relating to British exploits in Africa and these may be listed briefly; though they all have fascinating stories behind them:

Cape of Good Hope General Service Medal 1880–1897. The obverse shows a bust of Queen Victoria and the reverse the arms of Cape Colony. Only three bars were issued: Transkei, Basutoland, Bechuanaland. All these are scarce and only thirteen of the medals were awarded with all three bars.

British South Africa Company Medal 1890–1897. Victoria obverse and roaring lion hit by a spear reverse. There are four types of reverse with wording: Matabeleland 1893; Rhodesia 1896; Mashonaland 1897; and without place or date for the Mashonaland campaign 1890. Bars were awarded for: Mashonaland 1890; Matabeleland 1893, Rhodesia 1896 and Mashonaland 1897. The first engagement the recipient took part in was named on the reverse and the other actions were represented by bars.

Royal Niger Company Medal 1886–97. This medal has a flags and laurel-leaf reverse and was issued by the Company with Government approval. It was awarded for expeditions in the company's territories where casualties occurred. Silver medals were awarded to Europeans and bronze to natives. A bar 'Nigeria 1886–1897' was issued to Europeans and a bar 'Nigeria' to natives. The original medals had 'Spink and Son, Lond.' below the bust of Queen Victoria.

A number of the African medals are confusing to beginners because at first sight they appear identical. The East and West Africa Medal

1887–1900 has the same reverse as the Central Africa Medal which in turn is the same as the Ashanti Medal.

The East and West Africa Medal 1887–1900 was struck on a thinner flan to the Ashanti but is otherwise the same. It was issued with 21 bars and is normally found only with bars. The exception is MWELE, which is sometimes found impressed on one side of the claw:

1887–88	Brass River 1895
Witu 1890	1896–97
1891–92	1896–98
1892	Niger 1897
Liwondi 1893	Benin 1897
Witu August 1893	Dawkita 1897
Juba River 1893	1897–98
Lake Nyassa 1893	1898
1893–94	Sierra Leone 1898–99
Gambia 1894	1899
Benin River 1894	1900

East and Central Africa Medal 1897–1899. This medal has the same reverse as the Africa G.S. 1902 except that the words 'East and Central Africa' replace the word 'Africa'. It was mainly awarded for men employed in military expeditions in Uganda and for the Ogaden Somali war which lasted from April to August in 1898, also for actions in 1899 against Kabarega in Uganda.

Bars awarded were: Lubwas, Uganda 1897–98; 1898; Uganda 1899. It would be impossible to describe the individual actions, but to give an idea of the interest that some of these bars recall let us look at the actions in Uganda, often controlled by very small numbers of British soldiers relying on native and Sudanese troops who were likely to mutiny.

In 1897 Major Macdonald was given command of an expeditionary force which included the Uganda Rifles. These men had just come from an expedition involving 300 miles of marching and were now called upon to march another 350. In September the northward advance of the expedition was ordered with a view to finding out about the territories on the northern and eastern frontiers of East African and Uganda protectorates. At this the Sudanese troops mutinied and when intercepted by loyal troops, shots were fired.

The mutineers went to Fort Lubwas where Major Thruston and Mr

47

N. Wilson were in command, but the mutineers won over some of the garrison and the fort gates were opened to them. The Englishmen were overpowered and put in chains. Meanwhile Major Macdonald was on the track of the mutineers and caught up with them at Lubwas, on October 18. Heavy fighting began the next day and the mutineers committed themselves by shooting Major Thruston, Mr Wilson and another Englishman, Mr Scott, whom they had captured. Subsequently the mutineers suffered severe defeats but their mutiny made the local population feel that British rule was weak. This encouraged the dethroned King Mwanga to escape from custody in German territory, with a large force of undisciplined men, and Kabarega, the exiled king of Unyoro, came out in the open with his forces.

To subdue these kings meant many months of fighting in adverse conditions against superior numbers. The bars on this medal truly reflect human endeavour at its best.

Central Africa Medal 1891–1898. While having the same reverse as the East and West Africa Medal, this medal was issued with only one bar: 'Central Africa 1894–98'.

Boer War Medals. Medals of the Boer War are, at the moment, among the most inexpensive of all modern awards. They tell a fascinating story and mark the end of an era of warfare. It was the last major conflict involving British troops before World Wars I and II. It was the last war in which Britain could rely on volunteers—subsequent wars were on such a massive scale that conscription had to be brought in.

Many things changed in the Boer War. In the campaign against the Boers in 1881 it was found that the red uniforms of the British made good targets. This time the British fought in khaki.

When the war started in 1899 the military experts felt that a force of 50,000 could subdue the 'ignorant Boers'. They were so confident that the Queen's South Africa Medal was struck with the date 1899. In the event it needed many hundreds of thousands of soldiers and involved two years and eight months' continuous fighting. British deaths from all causes and those sent home as invalids amounted to the staggering total of 93,289 men and 4,188 officers. In addition 1,851 officers and 20,978 men were wounded in the war.

The date on the medal had to be erased—and only a few rare examples remain with the date in relief. Even so it can be seen quite clearly on close examination.

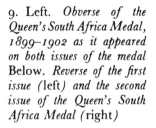

9. Left. *Obverse of the Queen's South Africa Medal, 1899–1902 as it appeared on both issues of the medal* Below. *Reverse of the first issue (left) and the second issue of the Queen's South Africa Medal (right)*

49

A total of 26 bars was issued for the medal which could also be awarded without bar in silver or bronze.

The bars were for:
Cape Colony
Natal
Rhodesia
Relief of Mafeking
Defence of Kimberley
Talana
Elandslaagte
Defence of Ladysmith
Belmont
Modder River
Tugela Heights
Relief of Kimberley
Paardeberg
Orange Free State
Relief of Ladysmith
Driefontein
Wepener
Defence of Mafeking
Transvaal
Johannesburg
Laing's Nek
Diamond Hill
Wittebergen
Belfast
South Africa 1901
South Africa 1902

10. *Reverse of Queen's South Africa Medal with bars for South Africa and Cape Colony*

While most of these are easy to obtain there are one or two rare ones like Defence of Mafeking, Wepener and Rhodesia.

Medals can be found with as many as eight bars and it is quite common to find them with three or four. In some cases a medal with one bar can be extremely rare, such as the Defence of Kimberley. Collectors set out to obtain the 26 bars and then develop the collection to include the various regiments, etc. at particular battles.

Apart from the Queen's South Africa Medal, collectors of this period will find the Queen's Mediterranean Medal 1899–1902 which was awarded to garrisons in the Mediterranean, and the King's South Africa Medal 1901–1902. This was issued with two bars 'South Africa 1901' and 'South Africa 1902'.

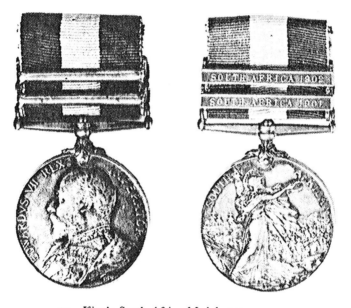

11. *King's South Africa Medal, 1901–2*

Two items collectors will also come across, although these are not campaign medals, are the Defence of Kimberley Star and Medal.

CHAPTER 5

INDIA

The Nepal War Medal 1814-1816

B Y General Order of March 20, 1816 this medal was granted to native soldiers and shows as an obverse design the hilly country of Nepal with guns and military fortifications. Main events of this war were the battles of Mukwampore and Sierapore, following which, the Rajah of Nepal came to terms with the British, and signed a treaty on March 4, 1816. Even with the excellent opportunities offered him during the Indian Mutiny, the Rajah remained true to his treaty and very soon the famous Gurkhas were fighting under British colours and to this day hold the record for the greatest number of Victoria Crosses to any unit.

In 1818 the Ceylon Medal was awarded to 45 men who had distinguished themselves during the Rebellion. The recipient's name was engraved on the reverse side of the medal and the issue was authorized by the Ceylon Government. This was followed in 1826 with the Burma Medal with the attractive elephant of Ava design. The reverse shows General Campbell at the storming of the Rangoon Pagoda. About 24,000 medals were issued in silver to native troops by the Honourable East India Company and, for the first time, the Company introduced ribbons to their medals.

Army of India Medal 1799-1826

As with the Military General Service Medal, this was not authorized until many years after the battles were over. The Order of March 21, 1851, allowed the East India Company to grant the medal to all survivors. Again, like the Military General Service Medal, the dates on the medal bear no relation to the actual battles. The Army of India Medal is dated 1799-1826 but the earliest bar awarded was for Allighur which was fought on September 4, 1803. Bars on this medal were arranged differently to previous medals, the last battle award being nearest to the medal itself. A total of 21 bars was issued:

Allighur	1803	Kirkee	1817
Battle of Delhi	1803	Poona	1817
Assaye	1803	Kirkee and Poona	1817
Asseerghur	1803	Seetabuldee	1817
Laswarree	1803	Nagpore	1817
Argaum	1803	Seetabuldee and	
Gawilghur	1803	Nagpore	1817
Defence of Delhi	1804	Maheidpoor	1817
Battle of Deig	1804	Corygaum	1818
Capture of Deig	1804	Ava	1824–26
Nepaul	(1814–1816)	Bhurtpoor	1826

Two separate dies are known for this medal, one being struck at the Royal Mint and the other at Calcutta Mint. The latter is identified by a long hyphen between the dates.

The medal gives collectors another opportunity of specialization and forms an interesting part of history. The Maheidpoor bar (December 21, 1817) reflects the last really serious attempt on British Arms at that period in history by Indian forces. The armies of Holkar and Cheetoo made a united attack on the British at Maheidpoor on the banks of the Seepra on that day. While 174 British soldiers died the Indians were routed and lost all their artillery. The Holkars hastily sued for peace and the Pindartees were pursued vigorously and had no time to reform. Cheetoo himself was chased into the wild hills, his last camp being surprised and cut to pieces. But the British were denied the pleasure of getting him. His body was found near the fort of Asseerghur (for which a bar had been awarded for earlier battles in 1803), torn to pieces by a tiger, his horse still grazing nearby with a saddlebag full of jewels.

The new collector will find the stories behind each bar of equal fascination and that the real fun of collecting is in finding out the details.

Coorg, a province of India on the Malabar coast, was annexed to the Madras presidency and a few years later there was an uprising. The Coorg Medal (April–May 1837) was awarded with a reverse inscription 'For distinguished conduct and loyalty to the British Government', to native troops who remained loyal throughout the Canara uprising.

The Afghan Wars provide an interesting series of medals and recall the fierce tribesmen in the proximity of the North West Frontier. Afghanistan's first connection with British history did not come until 1809 when Napoleon was rumoured to be organizing a joint invasion of India.

The Shah Shujah, ruler of Kabul, was dethroned by internal warfare and in 1839 the international political situation was such that Britain decided to reinstate him as a ruler. Accordingly, an army of 21,000 men was assembled on the Indus and advanced on Kandahar through the Bolan Pass. The city fell to them and the Shah Shujah was crowned on May 8. The army then advanced on Ghuznee, and Lieutenant Durand (later General Sir Henry Durand) blew down the city gate, the enemy 'melting away'.

But the new ruler was hated, largely because he was a British puppet, and rebellion broke out suddenly and caught the British without preparations. The British envoy was murdered at a conference and the British garrison of over 4,500 were forced to retreat towards Jellalabad. Only one man got through, Dr Brydon, the rest perishing in the wild mountain passes, at the hands of the Afghans.

Jellalabad itself came under siege and it was not until September 1842 that General Pollock, after defeating Mahomed Khan, again led British troops into Kabul.

Having restored order and departed, the Shah Shujah had little time to enjoy his kingdom. He was assassinated and Dost Mahomed Khan restored to his former power. With some justification he joined the Sikhs in their revolt against the British in 1848—but the political situation became such that a 'friendly understanding' was reached and a treaty concluded in 1855.

It is not surprising that the Shah Shujah decided to have a medal struck for all those who took part in capturing Ghuznee for his rule, but as he was assassinated before the medals were delivered the Indian Government had to bear the cost. The medal shows the fortress of Ghuznee and, on the reverse, the recipient's name and the date July 23, 1839.

The General Order of October 4, 1842, issued in Simla, authorized the Kandahar, Ghuznee and Kabul Medals. The medals were all the same except for the reverses, having the head of Queen Victoria. The reverses show Ghuznee, Cabul, Kandahar; Candahar, Ghuznee, Cabul; Cabul.

54

A further medal was given for Jellalabad (November 12, 1841 to April 7, 1842). The first issue was badly made in Calcutta and a second issue was made in London with the 'Flying Victory' design (the first showed the word Jellalabad over a crown). Soldiers were permitted to exchange the Calcutta medals for the better London ones, but it is believed that only a few elected to do so, and the second type went mainly to next of kin, etc. who had not received the first issue.

A scarce medal of the First Afghan War is the Defence of Kelat-i-Ghilzie, which currently fetches around £150. Kelat-i-Ghilzie was a little fort between Kabul and Kandahar which became a vital link. Captain John Halkett Craigie commanded the small garrison of about 60 Europeans and 900 natives, of which the bulk were men of the Shah Shujah's regiment. They withstood a siege for four months until relieved by Major-General Nott, and a special medal was struck for them by General Order of October 4, 1842.

Those interested in compiling a collection of Afghan war medals will find many more opportunities to add to the collection. An arrangement was arrived at between the British and Russian governments in 1872 that Afghanistan was beyond the field of Russian influence, and the practical violation of this understanding in 1878, led to the Second Afghan War. The victories at Ali Musjid and Peiwar and the capture of Kandahar and Khelat-i-Ghilzie by Sir Donald Stewart placed all the important vantage points of Eastern Afghanistan in British hands, with the exception of Kabul. A treaty was made but its provisions were scattered to the winds by the murder of Sir L. Cavagnari, the British envoy in Kabul. Sir F. Roberts advanced on the capital and inflicted a severe defeat on the inhabitants.

The Second Afghan War Medal (1878–1880) shows Queen Victoria's head on the obverse and a most attractive reverse design of an elephant carrying artillery followed by lancers.

Six different bars were issued which reflect the major battles necessary to subdue the fierce Afghans. Ali Musjid (November 21, 1878); Peiwar Kotal (December 2, 1878); Charasia (October 6, 1879); Kabul (December 10–23, 1879); Ahmed Khel (April 19, 1880); Kandahar (September 1, 1880).

At a time when the war seemed to be going well for the British, Abdur Rahman was proclaimed Amir. Ayoub Khan disputed this and led a revolt using all the tribes in Herat. General Burrows went out from Kandahar to deal with him but the British received a shock defeat at Maiwand and retired to Kandahar, where Ayoub Khan put the city under siege.

General Roberts then marched from Kabul to relieve Kandahar. It was a memorable march which required all the skill of a masterly leader: it succeeded and the Gurkhas and Seaforth Highlanders in particular distinguished themselves in the 300-mile march and total rout of the forces under Ayoub Khan at Kandahar.

Not surprisingly, a special award was made: the Kabul to Kandahar Star (August 9–31, 1880). Shortly after this the political situation was such that all British troops were able to be withdrawn and Abdur Rahman ruled with absolute British recognition.

The Afghan wars spread over many years and saw much desperate fighting. Many units took part and the various campaigns can be traced, battle by battle, through the medals of the men who made history.

While Britain was busily engaged in the Afghan problems in the 1840s the Scinde principalities in the lower valley and delta of the Indus, ruled over by the Ameers, caused trouble. A tribute had been enforced on them in 1839 and secretly they supported the Afghans.

When the British suffered reverses it emboldened some of the Ameers to take direct action. Sir Charles Napier was sent to Scinde to investigate and became violently prejudiced against the Ameers. To show his power Sir Charles captured Emangurb, a fort previously thought to have been invincible. Harsh treaty clauses were imposed and led to Beloochee troops attacking the Residency at Hyderabad, forcing Major Outram and his men to retreat to an armed steamer in the river.

Sir Charles Napier now marched in full battle order on Hyderabad and came up with the Beloochee army at Meeanee on February 17, 1843. He defeated them and went on to make a decisive victory near Hyderabad on March 22, 1843.

Scinde Campaign Medals were awarded, bearing the head of Queen Victoria and the name of the battle on the reverse. Three different medals were issued, bearing the reverses: Meeanee; Hyderabad; and Meeanee and Hyderabad, all dated 1843.

Lt.-Col. Pennefather, who led the 22nd Foot at Meeanee, had the steel suspenders of the medals to his regiment removed and replaced them with silver suspenders at his own expense. The 22nd Foot distinguished itself in the campaign to the extent that on return to its Bombay base the entire garrison was paraded to salute the regiment. During the campaign an eight-day march was made across desert territory, the guns being pulled along by foot soldiers.

The complete subjugation of the country followed and the Ameers were 'pensioned off' at Benares. Sir Charles Napier said of the whole affair, "We have no right to seize Scinde, yet we shall do so, and a very advantageous, useful and humane piece of rascality it will be."

The Gwalior Campaign Stars of 1843 recall that British rule in India had to be continually under force of arms. The fortress of Gwalior had first been taken by Major Popham in 1780 but in 1784 was recovered by the Scindiah. In 1804 it was again taken by the English under Sir H. White but was restored to the Scindiah the following year. When the reigning Scindiah died in 1843 the quarrels which broke out led to the British again intervening to restore order. The British defeated the Gwalior army at Maharajpoor and Punniar. Both actions were fought on the same day so the stars could not both be won by a soldier and are worded either 'Punniar' or 'Maharajpoor' with the date 1843. The stars were made from metal taken from captured guns.

Two years later the British had more trouble in India, this time with the Sikhs who invaded the Punjab with a 100,000-strong army. Sir Hugh Gough marched 150 miles to meet them and in quick succession delivered four major defeats upon the invading army, at Moodkee (December 18, 1845), Ferozeshuhur (December 21, 1845), Aliwal (January 28, 1846) and Sobraon (February 10, 1846) which compelled the Sikhs to seek a treaty.

The medal reverse shows Victory with the legend 'Army of the Sutlej' written around the circumference. There are four different exergues which can be collected. The wording is: Moodkee 1845; Ferozeshuhur 1845; Aliwal 1846; Sobraon 1846. The medal is unique in that the first battle the recipient took part in is named in the exergue and other battles by bars, it thus being possible for a soldier only to have three bars to the medal, the fourth possible battle being named in the exergue instead. This was also the first medal with bars which was awarded to both officers and men.

With hardly a break the British were fighting again in India from September 1848 to March 1849 in the Punjab Campaign, started when the proud Sikhs arose from national indignation and humiliation imposed from the Sutlej Campaign. It was but a repetition of the last campaign—and after three major defeats the Sikhs surrendered. The medal awarded for this campaign has a reverse design of Major-General Sir Walter Gilbert on horseback receiving the surrender of the Sikhs and the wording 'To the Army of the Punjab'. Three bars were issued—Mooltan, Chilianwala and Goojerat.

Very hard to get are the medals to the 24th Foot with the bar 'Chilianwala', for here the regiment had 21 officers and 500 men killed or wounded.

It is perhaps a strange historical fact, but these same Sikhs who had suffered such devastating defeats at the hands of the British were destined within a decade to rally to aid the British and it can be fairly argued that the Indian Mutiny 1857–58 would have had a different result had it not been for the loyalty of the Sikhs. Some of the Indian Mutiny medals are among the less expensive of all war medals of this period and are worthy of inclusion in any collection because of the great historical events they represent.

New Enfield rifles had been introduced into India and the bullets were greased with the fat of beef or pork, and were thus rendered unclean for Mohammedan and Hindu alike. The Sepoys considered the fat was introduced with the sole object of destroying their caste. The mutiny flared up throughout India. Many British and Europeans were massacred. The Indian Mutiny Medal (1857–1858) shows the head of Queen Victoria on the obverse and Britannia and the British Lion with the word 'India' on the reverse. In the exergue are the dates 1857–1858. Five different bars were awarded for Delhi, Defence of Lucknow, Relief of Lucknow, Lucknow, and Central India. The Order states that the medal could be awarded to all persons who had taken up arms against the mutineers or who had been fired on by them. Some 290,000 medals were awarded.

The most difficult bar to obtain is that for the Defence of Lucknow. The Defence was carried out between June 29 and November 22, 1857. Sir Henry Lawrence, commanding the garrison, died and was replaced by Major-General Sir John Inglis. The first small relief force were also entitled to this bar.

The bar for Delhi (May 30 to September 14) represents the core of the Indian Mutiny. The British, consisting of English, Sikhs, Afghans and Gurkhas, besieged 30,000 mutineers, and a siege train was brought up with artillery. On September 8 the batteries opened up and on the 13th a breach was made. For six days fighting continued in the streets, the British giving no quarter to any man with weapons in his hands. Bahadur Shah, who set himself up as the Great Mogul King, fled to a tomb of Humayun outside the city where he was captured by Captain Hodson. His two sons were cut down as they were re-entering the city. It was the turning-point of the revolution with the head of the mutineers in British hands, and his direct successors dead.

A bar was also awarded for the Relief of Lucknow in November 1857 and a bar 'Lucknow' for those troops under Sir Colin Campbell who made the final assault in order to capture the city. The Central India bar was given to those who served with Major-General Sir Hugh Rose, Major-General Roberts and Major-General Whitlock in various actions.

Indian General Service Medal

Presumably it now became clear to the British that they were to have continuous trouble with the natives of India, for the next medal is the Indian General Service Medal (1854–1895) and major campaigns that previously merited medals of their own were now reduced to bars. There were no less than 23 of them, and some of these bars represented campaigns that were fought for five years or more.

The British Resident at Pegu was insulted openly and a British warship fired on. That was good enough for war and powerful British forces subdued the area, concluding hostilities with the capture of Myat-Toon in his stronghold at Donubyu. The bar 'Pegu' was awarded for action between March 28, 1852 and June 30, 1853.

Other bars were: 'Persia' (December 5, 1856 to February 8, 1857). Persians occupied Herat, the gateway to Afghanistan and British forces drove them out.

'Northwest Frontier' (December 3, 1849 to October 22, 1868). During this long period—not far off twenty years—the British had continual trouble in the Frontier regions and many punitive expeditions were carried out, including sixteen major ones.

'Umbeyla' (October 20 to December 23, 1863). A fanatical conspiracy broke out in 1863 among the Sittana and other Afghan hill

12. *Indian General Service Medal 1854–95*

tribes. General Neville Chamberlain was unable to subdue them and was himself badly wounded in a battle near Umbeyla. Sir Hugh Rose then advanced and General Garnock successfully assaulted Umbeyla. On Christmas Day, 1863, the war was at an end and British forces marched home.

'Bhootan' (December 9, 1864 to February 1866). In 1863 an embassy under the Hon. Ashley Eden was insulted and ill-treated. War was declared, ending with the Bhotias ceding frontier districts of Assam.

'Looshai' (December 9, 1871 to February 20, 1872). This bar recalls the days when a Briton abroad could expect military assistance if insulted—the 'gunboat policy'. A planter and his daughter were abducted and two columns of men under arms marched under Brigadier-General G. Bourchier, the Cachar Column, and yet another under Brigadier-General C. W. Brownlow. The Looshais quickly returned the captives and it has been said that only two shots were fired.

'Perak' (November 2, 1875 to March 20, 1876). Here the British resident was murdered and retribution followed quickly for the Ismail.

'Jowaki 1877–8' (November 9, 1877 to January 19, 1878). This territory lay between Peshawar and the Kohat Pass. For many years the Afridis caused no trouble but when the British began building a road through the heart of their country they took to arms. Two expeditions were necessary and the bar awarded also bore the date—the first bar to the Indian Medal to do so.

'Naga 1879–80' (December 1879 to January 1880). The Local Commissioner, Mr Damant, was murdered on October 14, 1879 and a punitive expedition was launched against the Nagas.

'Burma 1885–7'; 'Burma 1887–9'; 'Burma 1889–92'. In the autumn of 1885 the oppressive attitude of the mad King Theebaw towards British merchants led to a war. A force of nearly 15,000 soldiers under General Prendergast was sent up the Irrawaddy and entered Mandalay on November 28. Theebaw was deposed but his brother led guerrilla bands—dacoits. The fighting against the dacoits went on for years and the bars were divided up to periods of years that a soldier was engaged in.

'Sikkim 1888' (March 15 to September 27). The Tibetans asked the Rajah of Sikkim, who effectively blocked the approaches to Tibet, to build a fort at Lingtu. This was against British trade-route interests and a force was dispatched which quickly occupied the new fort and destroyed it. But the Tibetans began constructing another fort in the Jelapla Pass so the expedition returned to deal with that. At the last battle the Tibetans had heavy casualties and returned to their own land.

'Hazara 1888' (October 3 to November 9). Known as the Black Mountain Expedition, Major-General J. W. McQueen led troops against the Black Mountain tribes after the murder of two British officers who had been surveying in the area. During one action British troops had to climb the Gorapher Peak, nearly 10,000 feet, while pursuing tribesmen.

'Chin Lushai 1889–90'. Again, this bar was for punitive expeditions. Two such expeditions were mounted, one against the Chins and the other against the Lushais. Few soldiers who took part in the actions remembered them with pleasure—they were fighting in thick, uncharted jungle most of the time.

'Samana 1891'. Syed Mir Basha, a priest, aroused the inhabitants by proclaiming 'jihad'—a holy war against unbelievers. British forces obliged him.

'Hazara 1891' (March 12 to May 16). Awarded to the Hazara Field

Force whose duties were mainly protecting the road building against Hassanzais tribesmen.

'N.E. Frontier 1891' (March 28 to May 7). Mr J. W. Quinton, Chief Commissioner for Assam, was murdered with other officers who after a short engagement had gone forward to negotiate with the Manipuris. British forces were sent up in three columns and on reaching Manipur found the heads of the officers in the Palace gardens.

'Hunza 1891'. Continued attacks on road construction in the area led to soldiers being sent to deal with the situation.

'Hunza Nagar Badge 1891'. This was not a bar but a badge 1 in. by $1\frac{1}{10}$ in. in size showing a hill fort and soldiers storming it. Really it was an additional award to the Hunza 1891 bar; it was given by the Maharajah of Jammu and Kashmir to Imperial Service troops who fought in the Hunza Nagar Expedition.

'Lushai 1889–92' (January 11, 1889 to June 8, 1892). Five expeditions were sent to the Lushai Hills and service in any one of these entitled the soldier to the bar.

'Chin Hills 1892–93' (October 19, 1892 to March 10, 1893). Awarded for punitive expeditions under Brigadier-General Palmer against the Chins.

'Kachin Hills 1892–93'. Awarded for punitive expeditions into the Kachin Hills.

'Waziristan 1894–95' (October 22, 1894 to March 13, 1895). The Waziris launched a series of attacks on the Afghan frontier and a large force had to be sent to deal with them.

In 1896 a new Indian General Service Medal, dated 1895, was brought into use. The reverse design shows a British soldier and a native soldier clasping a flag. This medal was to last to the end of the reign of Queen Victoria and six bars were awarded in that period. When Edward VII came to the throne his uniformed bust replaced that of Queen Victoria on the medal and among slight modifications to the reverse design was the deletion of the date '1895'. Only one bar was awarded to the medal, making this particular Indian General Service Medal cover the period 1895–1902.

Two of the bars relate to Chitral. Britain had just settled its difficulties in India when this small State caused trouble. The reigning Mehtar having murdered most of his rivals to the throne, was shot dead on orders of his half-brother while out hawking. The British Agent,

Surgeon-Major Robertson, decided to step in when the situation became even more complicated with the arrival of a Pathan free-booter, Urma Khan of Jandul, at the head of a strong force and marching in the name of Sher Afzul, an exiled uncle of the Mehtar. Sher Afzul was popular in the State. Robertson decided to ignore the lot and recognize a child as provisional Mehtar. He was engaged in battle and suffered considerable losses and was besieged in the Chitral Fort.

Colonel Kelly tried to force the snow-covered passes between Gilgit and Chitral and large relief forces had to be organized. On April 3 some 12,000 of the enemy held their own for some time until a cavalry charge by the Guides cavalry and the 11th Bengal Lancers broke their order.

Even so the Chitralis and the Pathans fought on and when the Guides crossed a ford under cover fire from the Highlanders and Borderers they were severely mauled, their Commanding Officer, Colonel Battye being killed.

The small band of men in the Chitral Fort held out for forty-seven days before being relieved.

The bar for 'Defence of Chitral 1895' is thus very rare, there being only about 500 men involved. (The Maharajah of Jammu and Kashmir also presented a medal, the Jammu and Kashmir Medal, to the native troops at the defence of Chitral.)

The 'Relief of Chitral' bar is a fairly common bar and testified to the large number of troops required to subdue the Pathan and Chitral forces. It was awarded for service under five different Commanding Officers who led their forces between March 7 and August 15.

Trouble flared up on the Punjab Frontier in June 1897 and scattered engagements resulted in a special bar 'Punjab Frontier 1897-98' being awarded.

13. *Indian General Service Medal 1936–39*

More insurrection led to bars for 'Malakand 1897' and 'Samana 1897', the final bar for the Victoria obverse being 'Tirah 1897–98', awarded to the Tirah Expeditionary Force.

The fighting in this last campaign became unusually tough for the British, and the situation at Dargai was only saved by one of the most famous frontal attacks in history. Colonel H. H. Mathias, commanding the Gordon Highlanders, addressed his men, "Men of the Gordon Highlanders . . . the General says that position must be taken at all costs. The Gordon Highlanders will take it!" With that he led the way. Four officers and 181 soldiers were killed but Dargai was taken. Every regiment engaged cheered the Gordons as they marched back to camp. Naturally medals to the Gordons are highly prized.

Queen Victoria died in 1901 and in that year trouble which broke out in the Mahsud and Waziri areas resulted in the bar 'Waziristan 1901–2.'

The Indian General Service Medal 1908–1935 had twelve bars and shows the fort at Jamrud overlooking the Khyber Pass as the reverse design. There were two issues of the medal, the first showing an obverse portrait of King Edward VII and the second the crowned head of King George V.

'The British had almost continual problems, the bars awarded being:

> North West Frontier 1908
> Abor 1911–12
> Afghanistan North West Frontier 1919
> Mahsud 1919–20
> Waziristan 1919–21
> Malabar 1921–22
> Waziristan 1921–24
> Waziristan 1925
> North West Frontier 1930–31
> Burma 1930–32
> Mohmand 1933
> North West Frontier 1935

Most of these bars are inexpensive by comparison to earlier medals and they can form an interesting collection. However, one of the bars, 'Waziristan 1925', is probably the hardest to get of all Indian General Service bars. This was awarded only to RAF personnel who served under Wing Commander Pink against the Waziris and marks the first occasion that the RAF was used as an attacking force completely unsupported by any other arm of the fighting forces.

The last Indian General Service Medal was for the years 1936–39 when such frontier campaigns became overshadowed by the world war which broke out and embraced all servicemen. The two bars issued were both for the North West Frontier and bear the dates 1936–37 and 1937–39 respectively. The reverse design shows a tiger, while the head of George VI is on the obverse. There were two strikings of the medal, one by the Royal Mint and one in Calcutta, the latter being inferior to a degree that the lack of workmanship is easily noticeable, particularly when looking at the tiger's claws.

Those collectors of the medals awarded for service in India will find other more recent medals like the Indian Independence Medal (though not a campaign medal), and the Indian Service Medal 1939–45 which was awarded to forces who had three years' non-operational service in India.

CHAPTER 6

CHINA

BRITISH problems in China resulted in no less than three wars and for each of these a medal was struck. The China War medals form a compact group which enable specialists to produce collections tracing the great historical events of this period.

The problems may be said to have begun when the exclusive right of the East India Company to trade with China ceased on April 22, 1834. With the opening of general trade came smuggling and piracy, particularly associated with opium. Commissioner Lin, as Imperial Commissioner, required all opium to be destroyed and Captain Elliot arranged for some 20,282 chests of opium to be delivered to the Chinese for destruction. But Lin then issued an Imperial edict to the effect that all trade with Britain should cease.

Captain Elliot blockaded the river at Canton and took the island of Chusan. The sufferings of Britain's forces can be gauged by the fact that one in four died of disease.

Canton was held to a ransom of £1,250,000, which at first the Chinese showed no signs of paying. But when Sir Henry Pottinger succeeded Captain Elliot the Chinese suffered a series of quick military defeats and in addition to the ransom were required to pay an indemnity of nearly four and a half million pounds. At the same time, by the Treaty of Nanking in 1842, the Chinese agreed to give the island of Hong Kong to the British.

Although only a 'little war' it secured trade between China and the West and Hong Kong is today the only link with Communist China. The men who made it all possible were awarded a medal known to collectors as the First China War Medal. On the obverse is the head of Queen Victoria and the reverse has a design of war trophies with the royal arms in an oval shield. Originally it had been intended that the design would show a lion defeating a dragon in battle. But it was decided that this would cause the Chinese to lose 'too much face' so the war-trophy design was used. The war lasted from July 5, 1840 to August 1842. It was awarded for the capture of Chusan and for various engagements in the Canton river. The capture of Nanking ended the war and the words 'Nanking 1842' appear in the exergue of the medal.

For a time affairs with China were reasonably peaceful but in 1855 the cutter *Arrow* was seized by the Chinese and charged with piracy. This was the cause of the Second Chinese War.

There was little doubt that the vessel was acting highly suspiciously, however, it had a British registration and Sir John Bowering demanded the surrender of the captured men. The Chinese handed them over but refused to apologize and Canton was immediately bombarded. The Taku Forts were taken in 1858, but had to be taken again in 1860 after Sir F. Bruce was fired upon while sailing past them. The Chinese submitted when their capital, Peking, was threatened.

The medal for the Second China War has a reverse design of war trophies and the word 'China' in the exergue. Six bars were awarded:

China 1842
Canton 1857
Fatshan 1857
Taku Forts 1858
Taku Forts 1860
Pekin 1860

More trouble came in 1900 and the Third China War started. It was quick and decisive, lasting from June to December, 1900. Three bars were awarded for the special medal for the Third China War—Taku Forts, Defence of Legations and Relief of Pekin.

The anti-foreign, or Boxer movement, as it was known, had become dangerous and when native Christians were massacred a small force of 340 marines and sailors was sent to guard the legations in Peking. When it was realized how critical the situation was, Admiral Sir Edward Seymour headed a relief force of about 2,000 men and marched along the railway line from Taku to Peking. He was intercepted by well-armed Boxers and was forced to retire.

More forces were amassed but early in July things looked very black, with the Chinese having an estimated 140,000 troops in the capital. Indeed, the Allied commanders decided at one stage that Peking should

14. *China Medal 1900. This display was of medals to warships. Notice that many did not receive bars. Only two of the medals in the display have bars, both for the "Relief of Pekin"*

be left to its fate. *The Times* wrote: "For the moment civilization confesses itself important in the face of barbarism".

Japan was asked to help, having forces near at hand. Many countries sent troops and the fighting became vicious as the Boxers were quelled. Collectors look for bars to soldiers who particularly distinguished themselves, such as the two squadrons of Bengal lancers who charged the Tartar cavalry and captured their standards.

Peking fell to the allies, and, in what was probably the last event of its kind in modern history, was sacked and plundered by eight nations whose forces captured it. The Dowager-Empress escaped by the western gate.

During the sacking of the town British soldiers upturned a statue of the Buddha and found underneath it the earliest paper money that has come to light in any quantity, the Ming notes of the fourteenth century —put there in the manner that we put items under foundation stones.

The Chinese wars make an enthralling story and even a few medals with different bars can unfold the story of Britain's Chinese troubles over a period of 60 years.

CHAPTER 7

OTHER THEATRES OF WAR

The Crimea

THE Crimean War has gone down in history for the famous Charge of the Light Brigade—though as medal collectors know, the Charge of the Heavy Brigade was just as gallant, and more rewarding for the British; also because it drew attention to the terrible circumstances of the troops and lack of help for the wounded. It was a turning-point in attitudes towards fighting men.

A fine subject for the specialist collector, there were some 275,000 Crimea War Medals issued. Five bars were issued also: Alma, Balaklava, Inkermann, Sebastopol and Azoff, but it was only possible for any one person to obtain four bars.

The last awarded bar was worn nearest to the actual medal, in other words, in reverse order of receiving the bars.

Azoff was a naval battle, the others being land battles and all of great importance.

Medals to soldiers committed to battle on October 25 are valued highly by all collectors, particularly those awarded to the Heavy Brigade (around £40), the Light Brigade (around £100) and the 93rd Foot (around £30).

The Charge of the Light Brigade is so famous that little need be said about it, though the Charge of the Heavy Brigade has been recorded by an eye witness, Mr W. H. Russell of *The Times*:

"All was visible to the men and officers on Mount Sapoune. They sat or stood, French and British, looking down with breathless interest on the scene below. They saw the Russian horse, nearly 3,000 strong, sweep majestically over the rising ground . . . and the little squadrons of the Heavy Brigade, which altogether did not equal a fifth of the force swooping down upon them. As the Russians rolled over the ridge, they instinctively fronted towards the tiny squadrons. They advanced down

70

15. *British Crimea Medal 1854–56*

the hill at a slow canter, which they changed to a trot at last nearly halted. The first line was nearly double the length of ours, and it was at least three times as deep. The trumpets rang out through the valley, and the Greys and Enniskilliners went right at the centre of the Russian cavalry. Turning a little to their left so as to meet the Russian right, the Greys rushed on with a cheer that thrilled every heart. The wild shout of the Enniskilliners rose through the air at the same instant. As lightning flashes through a cloud, the Greys and Enniskilliners pierced through the dark masses of Russians. The shock was but for a moment. There was a clash of steel, and a light play of sword blades in the air.

71

16. *Sultan of Turkey's Crimea Medal 1854–56—Sardinian version*

In another moment we saw them emerging with diminished numbers and in broken order, charging against the second line. In less than five minutes 700 British swordsmen had beaten 3,000 Russian horse.''

Small wonder that collectors pay high prices for medals to those men. The same goes for the Guards at Inkermann, firmly placed in British history by the famous painting by Robert Gibb 'Saving the Colours: the Guards at Inkermann'. At Alma it was the Highland Brigade which distinguished itself so greatly: ''The Highlanders coming up in succession from the right, smote each column in flank as it passed its front, while every moment the rigid line of red coats and black bearskins and busy rifles crept closer and closer . . .''

Naturally medals to the units which achieved such distinction are very expensive, but medals to soldiers who fought hard and well are still available for as little as £5.

Collectors of this campaign can also obtain Turkish Crimea Medals. This award has three different obverses, in which the national flags are placed in different order and the words in the exergue read: 'Crimea 1855' (British); 'La Crimée 1855' (French) and 'La Crimea 1855' (Sardinian).

New Zealand Medal 1845–1847 and 1860–1866

Queen Victoria's head appears on the obverse of this scarce medal with a wreath on the reverse with the words, 'New Zealand—Virtutis Honor'. It was authorized in 1869. It is unusual in that while no bars were issued the dates of service of the recipient were engraved inside the wreath. So far 28 different dates have been recorded, and the medal was also issued undated.

It went to soldiers and sailors engaged against the Maori uprising between 1845 and 1847, and for the later Maori campaign which lasted six years from 1860 to 1866 when the Maori warriors were finally crushed. The undated medal is the only one commonly met with— fetching around £11. The other medals fetch anything from £25 to well over £100. The medals were named by impressed capitals.

Known dates:

1845–46	1861–65
1845–47 (probably Navy only)	1861–66
1846–47 Navy only	1862–66
1846 Navy	1863
1847 Navy	1863–64
1848 only one known to Army	1863–65
1860 Navy	1863–66
1860–61	1864
1860–63	1864–65
1860–64	1864–66
1860–65	1865
1860–66	1865–66
1861	1866
1861–63	Undated
1861–64	

Canada

Riel's Rebellion in 1885 gave rise to the North West Canada Medal. No British troops took part in the campaign which was awarded to

73

Canadian troops by the Canadian Government. Fierce fighting took place in the area of the Saskatchewan Rivers and a bar—'Saskatchewan'—was issued for these engagements. The medal shows Victoria's head on the obverse and on the reverse it has a maple wreath with the words: 'North West Canada' and the date '1885'.

The Canada General Service Medal was issued for the period 1866–70, but was not authorized until 1899. It was awarded to British soldiers and Canadian militia during the Fenian Raids of 1866–70, and the famous Red River expedition in 1870.

Three bars were issued:

    Fenian Raid 1866
    Fenian Raid 1870
    Red River 1870

The crowned and veiled head of Victoria is depicted on the obverse. The reverse design shows the Canadian flag inside a maple wreath. The medal ribbon was later also used for the Canada Medal (1943) the first Canadian decoration for 'meritorious service above and beyond the faithful performance of duties'.

Tibet

The Tibet Medal (1903–04) is rare to British troops and was awarded to troops engaged in the Tibet Mission who were at Siliguri between December 13, 1903 and September 23, 1904. The reverse shows the hilltop fortress of Lhasa with the legend 'Tibet 1903-4' below. One bar—'Gyantse'—was issued for a battle which was fought between May 3 and July 6, 1904. The naming on these medals is by engraved script and unofficial bars exist. Issued in both silver and bronze, they are all rare.

British North Borneo Medals 1897–1937

Forces employed by the British North Borneo Company were awarded company medals which had the authority of the British Government. The Medal for Punitive Expeditions 1897–8, has the arms of the Company with a Jacobean shield and a six-oared galley on the obverse. The design is supported either side by a wild man of Borneo. The reverse shows the British lion and the flag of the colony.

74

They were issued with three bars:

> Punitive expedition (1897)
> Punitive expeditions (1897–98)
> Rundum (1915–16)

The Medal for Tambunan (1899–1900) has an obverse design of the company's coat of arms and a reverse showing the company's flag. It was awarded to forces taking part in the Tambunan expedition and for capturing Mat Saleh's fort.

The Rundum Medal (1915–16) was issued with bar 'Rundum' but those with previous medals wore only the bar 'Rundum' to their existing medal. Only 113 such medals were awarded.

A General Service Medal was also issued and was awarded up until 1937.

General Service Medal 1918–62

This medal underwent six changes to its obverse design, all having a common reverse design of the winged figure of Victory.

1. King George V. Legend: GEORGIVS V BRITT: OMN: REX ET IND: IMP.
2. King George V. Legend: GEORGIVS V D.G. BRITT OMN REX ET INDIAE IMP.
3. King George VI. Legend: GEORGIVS VI D.G. BR. OMN. REX ET INDIAE IMP.
4. King George VI. Legend: GEORGIVS VI DEI GRA: BRITT: OMN: REX: FID: DEF.
5. Queen Elizabeth. Legend: ELIZABETH II DEI GRA: BRITT: REGINA: F.D.
6. Queen Elizabeth. Legend: ELIZABETH II DEI GRATIA REGINA F.D.

Bars awarded:

> Kurdistan
> Iraq
> N.W. Persia
> S. Persia
> Southern Desert: Iraq.

17. United Nations Service Medal 1950–

Northern Kurdistan
Palestine
South East Asia 1945–46
Bomb and Mine Clearance 1945–49
Bomb and Mine Clearance 1945–56
Palestine 1945–48
Malaya
Cyprus
Near East
Arabian Peninsula
Brunei

Modern Medals

Medals were issued for the Korean War 1950–53, the British issue being in cupro-nickel and the Canadian issue in silver. The two scarce medals of this war are the South African issue and the Southern

76

Rhodesia issue. Most commonly met with is the United Nations bronze award.

The current General Service Medal came into being in 1962 and is used for all three arms of the fighting forces. The bars awarded so far are:

Borneo
Radfan
South Arabia
Malay Peninsular
South Vietnam

CHAPTER 8

THE TWO WORLD WARS

W ORLD WAR I was the last war in which, for a time, Britain could rely on volunteers. When casualties began to mount it was necessary to enforce conscription. Even though World War II was to be a larger war with more casualties overall, for the British World War I was the more serious, with hundreds of thousands of casualties in a matter of months.

Anyone who received the 1914 Star certainly earned it. This award was in the form of a three-point star, the top ending in a crown. Two swords cross in the centre with a scroll and the date '1914'. This went to forces under Field-Marshal Sir J. D. P. French who commanded the early stages of the war. A bar '5th August–22nd November, 1914' was also issued, for those personnel who served under fire between August 5, 1914 and 23 November, 1914.

18. *1914 Star*

An identical star except for the dates in the scroll, which now changed to '1914–15', was issued for subsequent operations between the dates August 5, 1914 and December 31, 1915. Recipients' names were in block capitals on the reverse of the stars.

The British War Medal 1914–1918 has a reverse design of St George trampling on the shield of the central powers, with a skull and cross-bones below. Issued in silver and bronze with naming in small indented block capitals round the edge, the medal was given to all personnel who served between August 5, 1914 and November 11, 1918.

19. *First World War medals*
Above. *British War Medal 1914–18*   Below. *Allied Victory Medal 1914–19*

79

The Victory Medal was issued in bronze and had an obverse design of the winged figure of Victory. On the reverse in the centre of a wreath are the words: 'The Great War for Civilisation 1914–1919'.

An interesting medal of the Great War is the Territorial Forces' War Medal 1914–19. The reverse legend has around the top: 'Territorial War Medal' and the words 'For Voluntary Service Overseas 1914–19' inside a wreath. It was awarded to the famous Territorials who completed not less than four years service before August 4, 1914 or who were serving on that date, provided they rejoined by September 30, 1914. As this award was not given to those who qualified for the 1914 or 1914–15 stars, it is a comparatively scarce award.

20. *Territorial Force War Medal 1914–19*

There was also the Mercantile Marine War Medal 1914–18 and the South African issue of the Victory Medal.

With well over 50 belligerent nations World War II was fought on a scale so massive that it was quite out of the question to engrave the names of recipients on the war medals for campaigns. Some collectors specialize in World War II and try and get one of each type of medal issued by the nations of both sides. It becomes a formidable collection.

The British medals are generally inexpensive because of the large number of forces taking part. Perhaps the scarcest of all is the Air Crew Europe Star which fetches around £7.

In all there were eight campaign stars. While they do not bear the recipient's name, unless privately engraved, they nevertheless relate to some of the most momentous happenings in the history of the world.

The 1939–45 Star (six-pointed star with Royal cypher surmounted by crown superimposed on a circlet with the words 'The 1939–1945 Star') was awarded generally for six months' operational service, or a lesser period in specific actions. A bar was issued for those who flew fighters in the Battle of Britain between July 10 and October 31, 1940.

The Atlantic Star (same as 1939–45 star but with words 'The

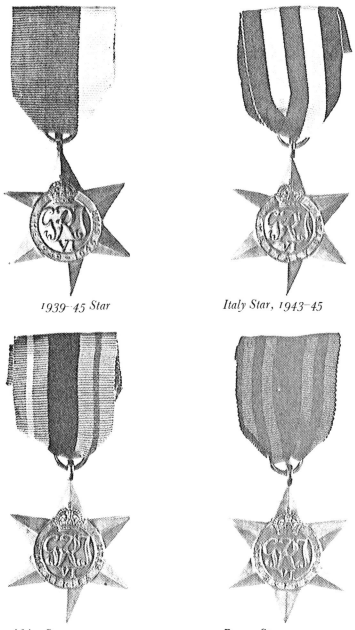

1939–45 Star   *Italy Star, 1943–45*

Africa Star, 1940–43   *Burma Star, 1941–45*

21. *Four Second World War Medals*

Atlantic Star') was awarded to those who served in Atlantic operations. There were various qualifications but generally it was for 360 days' operational service at sea or 120 days' service with aircrew. It followed that the recipient was also entitled to the 1939–45 Star. Two bars, France and Germany, and Air Crew Europe were issued, but only one could be worn, as the star of the first received was awarded instead.

Air Crew Europe Star was issued under the same conditions for bars, both Atlantic and France and Germany being available, but only one could be worn. This star was for personnel engaged in operational flying from the United Kingdom over Europe from September 3, 1939 to June 5, 1944.

Africa Star. Bars issued for this star were '8th Army', '1st Army', and 'North Africa 1942–43'. Only one bar could be worn to the Star. The recipient had to serve in North Africa during the period from June 10, 1940 to May 12, 1943.

Pacific Star. One bar: 'Burma'. Issued for service between December 8, 1941 and September 2, 1945 in the Pacific. The Pacific Star was an alternative award to the Burma Star so the recipient could only wear one. If he had served in both theatres he could wear the bar of the other.

Burma Star. Bar: 'Pacific'. The Burma campaign lasted from December 11, 1941 to September 2, 1945. In certain cases this award also went to servicemen who were in China, Malaya, and Sumatra.

Italy Star. For the purpose of the award the operational theatre included Sardinia, Greece, Corsica, Elba, Yugoslavia and Austrian territory. The operational dates were June 11, 1943 to May 9, 1945.

France and Germany Star. Bars: 'Atlantic' and 'Air Crew Europe'. Recipients who also qualified for Atlantic and Air Crew Europe were only allowed the first they were entitled to, the other was represented by a bar. Operational dates were June 6, 1944 to May 8, 1945.

The medals most commonly met with of the 1939–45 war are the Defence Medal and the War Medal 1939–45. The Defence Medal was issued to personnel engaged in non-operational service in the Armed Forces, such as Home Guard, Civil Defence, mine and bomb disposal units, etc. It needed three years' service to qualify in the United Kingdom, or 180 days' service overseas in a non-operational area subject to air attack, or one year's service in a completely non-operational area subject to air attack, or one year's service in a completely non-

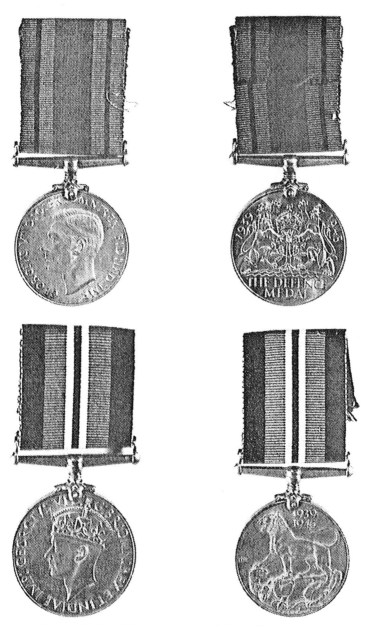

22. Above. *Defence Medal 1939–45*. Below. *War Medal 1939–45*

operational area overseas. The reverse design shows lions flanking the Crown.

The War Medal was awarded for full-time service during the period September 3, 1939 to September 2, 1945. Army personnel only had to serve for 28 days to qualify for the award. The reverse of the medal shows a lion standing on a dragon.

Both the Defence and War Medals were issued in pure silver to Canadian forces and are worth several times as much as the ordinary awards.

A number of Commonwealth medals were also issued. Again, most of these are fairly inexpensive except for the South Africa War Services Medal (Home and Voluntary Service) which fetches around £10.

These medals comprise: Indian Service Medal; Canadian Volunteer Service Medal—a bar was issued for this; Africa Service Medal (Overseas Service); South Africa War Services Medal (Home and Voluntary Service); New Zealand War Service Medal; Southern Rhodesia Service Medal; and Australian Service Medal.

CHAPTER 9

ORDERS AND DECORATIONS

No one is quite sure when orders and decorations in the modern sense of the words were first introduced but they can be traced to medieval times and were used by the Catholic Church.

An 'order' meant that a group of people agreed to a set of rules of behaviour and formed an association.

It did not take long for these 'orders' to take on a military cloak. With the advent of the Crusades some of the most famous orders were founded—and while ostensibly religious, they were in practice devoted to killing the enemies of the Christian religion.

Hugo de Payns, a French knight, founded the famous Order of the Knights Templars in 1118 and its members referred to themselves as 'Christi milites'—the Knights of Christ. Garbed in white mantles and the red cross of St George, they spent their time fighting the infidels. The Order was recognized by Pope Honorius the Second in 1123 and, when the Crusades were over, the Order spread its influence until it became so powerful it was a threat to the ruling powers.

King Philip the Fair of France outlawed the Order and its vast properties and wealth were confiscated, its members being hunted down and killed. The Grand Master, Jacques de Molay, was burned at the stake.

The Order of Malta was founded even earlier and its members wore a black cloak and white cross (Maltese) during war and a red cloak with Latin white cross during peace. After the Crusades (at which time they were known as the Order of St John of Jerusalem), the Order moved to Cyprus and then Malta, from which it derives its present name. The Knights of Malta reigned supreme for centuries until Napoleon destroyed their power in 1798. Today the Order has its headquarters in Rome and still exerts influence.

The Teutonic Order, although started as a hospital order, was undoubtedly one of the fire and sword. Duke Frederick of Swabia, commanding the German crusaders, formed the Order during the Siege of Acre in 1190. In Eastern Europe the Order gained control of Courland, Livonia and Estonia. In 1240 the Order was joined by the Knights of the Sword.

Its enormous power was swept away at the battle of Tannenberg when the combined forces of Poland and Lithuania defeated the Knights of the Teutonic Order (1410)—from then on it retreated and was finally abolished by Napoleon in 1809. Emperor Ferdinand I of Austria re-established the Order in 1839 and it was made a religious order by Pope Pius XI in 1929.

In the fourteenth century as royal power usurped the church authority, various temporal orders of chivalry were instituted. Meetings —or chapters—were held in places of worship but there the religious part of the Orders ended. Their prime purpose was to strengthen the hand of the king and in most cases he saw to it that he was the Grand Master himself. Membership was limited and noble birth was a requirement of membership. Some of these temporal orders still exist but today they are virtually used by royalty to bestow royal favour by granting membership. The greatest of these is probably the Order of the Garter founded in 1348 by King Edward III. It is said that when the Countess of Salisbury dropped a garter the King picked it up and to the laughing assembly said, 'Honi soit qui mal y pense' (Evil be to him who evil thinks) and adopted the garter for the Order of the Garter.

With the French Revolution, the idea of noble birth being a qualification for membership of an Order was dropped. Orders of Merit were introduced with five classes of the French Legion of Honour—instituted in 1802. At first it was purely a reward for military service but later was awarded to civilians for services to society.

The Orders which generally interest the collector of war medals are those which are purely military orders or are mixed orders in that they can be awarded for military and civilian divisions.

Some of the military orders still in existence were founded centuries ago, such as the Swedish Order of the Sword, 1522. Other famous orders are the Dutch Military Order of William which started in 1815, the Finnish Order of the Liberty Cross, 1918, which later was only awarded in times of war, the decoration itself being distinguished by swords for military awards as against civilian.

In the case of Mixed Orders the military division is shown by the addition of swords to the order. Well known orders in this category are the Order of Leopold (Belgium 1832), Order of St Olaf (Norway 1847), Order of Merit (Great Britain 1902), Order of the White Lion (Czechoslovakia 1922).

There are exceptions to the crossed swords and the Order of the British Empire has an extra band to the riband when awarded for military service. The Order of the Bath, instituted in 1725, has different insignia for each class.

The insignia consists of a number of different items. The Badge of the Order is usually the main symbol and is often in the form of a jewelled medallion, or a cross or a star. Then there is the Riband of the Order which is a woven silk ribbon with or without *moiré*. These are sometimes decorated with woven crosses, eagles, etc.

Stars of the Order vary between four- and twelve-pointed stars and are usually made of gold or silver. Until the twentieth century they were made of cloth and were worn on the cloaks.

23. *German First and Second World War Medals with Crossed Swords*

24. *Military Medal, George V*

The Collar of the Order is really a chain made of gold or silver and is designed in many instances to attach the Badge of the Order.

Then there is special insignia to an Order. These include 'with Oak Leaves' for German military Orders of the last war, and with many Orders it is 'palm leaves', 'stars' or 'crossed swords'.

Although this book is concerned with campaign medals, the collector will often come across groups of medals, and among them will sometimes be decorations. Naturally a group of medals to the same men which includes a decoration for a particular incident in a campaign greatly enhances the value.

The most coveted British decoration is the Victoria Cross. Instituted by Queen Victoria following the Crimean War, these medals are made from the bronze of captured guns. Today one can expect to have to pay £1,000 for a Victoria Cross.

The George Cross is the civilian counterpart of the Victoria Cross. It was introduced in 1940 and replaced the Medal of the Order of the British Empire for Gallantry. These Gallantry Orders were required to be exchanged for the new George Cross and are more common than the awards since 1940. Service awards are more valuable than civilian awards—servicemen could win the George Cross under certain circumstances. This also applies to the George Medal.

The Distinguished Service Order (DSO) was issued in gold for the first two or three years and as such is extremely rare. Later, it was changed to silver gilt. The most common of these awards are those of George V which fetch on average £30.

The Distinguished Service Cross (DSC) was first issued in 1901 as the Conspicuous Service Cross and became the DSO in 1914. The same award for non-commissioned officers and men was called the Distinguished Service Medal (DSM), and the Military Medal (MM) was awarded in large numbers during the Great War, so that collectors can obtain them for around £4. However, it is hard to find this decoration issued during the reign of Elizabeth II and it can cost more than £50.

The Distinguished Flying Medal (DFM) and the Air Force Medal (AFM) were issued specifically for the Air Force.

Other decorations to look for are:

Queen's (and King's) Police Medals for Gallantry and Distinguished Service.
Military Cross (MC).
Distinguished Flying Cross (DFC).
Air Force Cross (AFC).
Order of British India (OBI).
Indian Order of Merit.
The Kaiser-i-Hind Medal.
The Order of Burma.
Albert Medal.
Union of South Africa King's (Queen's) Medal for Bravery.
Conspicuous Gallantry Medal—Royal Navy.
Conspicuous Gallantry Medal—Royal Air Force.
Distinguished Conduct Medal (DCM).
Edward Medal.
Constabulary Medal—Ireland.
Sea Gallantry Medal.
Royal West African Frontier Force (DCM).

King's African Rifles (DCM).
Indian Distinguished Service Medal.
Queen's Fire Brigade Medals for Gallantry and Distinguished
  Service.
Foreign Office Medals.
Indian Police Medal for Gallantry.
Colonial Police Medal.

CHAPTER 10

NAMING OF MEDALS

Naming of Medals

THE majority of British campaign medals are named. That is to say the name of the recipient is to be found on the edge of the medal together with details of his rank and regiment. Medals awarded to officers are worth more than those awarded to other ranks simply because it is easier to trace the service records of officers, and find out what happened to them.

Naturally medals to senior ranks, like Admirals or Field Marshals are very much sought after because these are the men who influenced the course of battle and, more often than not, were ultimately responsible for the success or failure of a campaign.

So the new collector will quickly be aware that the name on the edge of a medal is very important. He must satisfy himself that a named medal in his possession is genuine. When one considers that a medal awarded to a private soldier in a major campaign may be worth three or four pounds, yet the same type medal awarded to a famous soldier may be worth a hundred pounds, it is realized that the unscrupulous forger has only to change the name on the medal, to make an excellent living. There are few medals which were forged as such, and most of those are easily detected. It is the naming which is difficult for the new collector.

First, it must be remembered there are some medals which were issued unnamed. This applies to all the campaign stars, etc, of World War II—because they were issued in such vast numbers it was not practical to name them all.

But earlier medals can also be found unnamed for various reasons. These include: Baltic, Burma 1826, Kandahar, Kabul, Crimea, China 1857, North-West Canada.

It is with these types of medals that the difficulties occur. Some of them, for instance, could be returned for official naming—as with the Crimea Medal. Many of them were semi-officially named. That is to say the colonel of the regiment would have them engraved at his own expense. Sometimes they would be engraved or impressed by local craftsmen in India, sometimes the recipient would take his medal to his home-town jeweller and have his name engraved on it.

All these are perfectly acceptable to a collector provided he knows they are genuine, and the circumstances of the naming.

But a common form of forgery is to 'rub-down' the edges of a medal to erase the name and then replace it with another name, such as one relating to a 'scarce' regiment.

This form of forgery is no trouble to an experienced collector who takes the trouble to 'know' his medals. By establishing the correct circumference of the medal he can, with a pair of callipers, measure the medal and detect if it has been rubbed down. Invariably, a medal so treated shows up in the places where the old name had once been, whereas the parts of the medal edge which had not been engraved remain true.

Occasionally the man's name will have been left alone but his rank or regiment altered. For this reason the callipers must be used to check the entire circumference.

Although that may sound straightforward, trouble will occur because sooner or later the collector comes across medals which have clearly been tampered with—yet may still be genuine.

People selling family medals sometimes rub the names off—not appreciating that they are destroying the main value of the medal. Someone who has lost a medal may buy another, erase the name and replace it with his own. Sometimes the rank will have been erased and replaced with another—often simply a sign that the owner was promoted.

A beginner would be well advised to accept only medals which are clearly named. The exceptions to the rule can come later when he is conversant with the possibilities.

The collector who specializes in certain campaign medals is better off than the general collector in that it is not too difficult to learn the type-faces used for naming medals in various campaigns.

He will soon be in a position to know that a certain medal should have the name 'impressed' rather than engraved in script. For example,

Waterloo medals are always impressed. Any such medal not impressed is a forgery.

Medals were also officially reissued in cases where the recipient lost the original. These days such medals are marked 'Duplicate' or 'Replacement', but it was not always so. This has led to two medals being in existence to the same man, and both genuine!

The other danger a collector has to be on guard against is tampering with the bars. It is not unknown for someone to take bars from one medal and add them to another to make it more valuable.

In such a case all the bars are genuine and the collector must check against the rolls to see if the recipient was entitled to those bars. Learning to detect such tamperings is not an easy task and until experienced it is better to leave suspicious medals well alone or only purchase them from reliable medal dealers who will vouch for their authenticity.

Bars have been forged too. Quite a few Boer War bars exist but fortunately, on being compared to the genuine bars they are easily detected.

Alec A. Purves, one of the leading experts on medals, has written an indispensable handbook for collectors wishing to check the types of naming and bars for each medal. His book, *Collecting Medals and Decorations*, is ideal for this purpose.

CHAPTER 11

DISPLAY

HALF the fun in collecting anything is to be able to set it out neatly and concisely so that a viewer can see it to the best advantage.

Medals allow many methods of display. For the ordinary purpose of filing a collection until it can be displayed properly, an envelope filing system can be used, bearing in mind that each medal should be individually wrapped so as to prevent rubbing or knocking against other medals. Remember that whatever the state the medal was in when acquired, once in your possession it should not be allowed to deteriorate. Do not be taken in by the few dealers who use sales jargon to the effect that worn medals are better because it proves they were actually worn. This is rubbish, as is the other favourite expression, 'you would be worn a bit too if you were a hundred years old'. Collectors look for perfection in the item they are collecting, and just so long as such items exist in perfection, that is the standard they are looking for.

So whatever filing system is adopted be sure that the medals cannot 'bang' together causing fresh scratch marks, and, of course, be sure that they are filed so that you can easily find what you are looking for.

Home-made trays or cabinets can be ideal for display, and special cabinets can be purchased. Do not overcrowd a tray, and in 'writing up' the collection remember the editorial dictum for caption writing: 'Don't say anything in the caption that is readily apparent in the picture'. In other words there is no need to write 'Obverse: Queen Victoria' if the portrait of Queen Victoria is staring the viewer in the face. Tell him something he cannot tell by looking at the medal, e.g. the number issued, the designer, etc. Medal ribbons add to the effect of the display.

There is little advantage in showing a tatty ribbon simply because it was the original. It is far better to replace it with a new, clean ribbon

25. *East and West Africa Medal (1887–1900). A collection showing the various bars awarded, including those to ships*

to give a better display effect. The old ribbon can always be filed away in case during a later exchange the other person likes to have original ribbons.

Medals are also ideally suited to be framed in picture frames and hung on the wall. For this purpose little tacks can be used to hold the medals in position, with a tiny pin through the ribbon for extra strength. This allows pictures of the battles, etc, to be displayed in the frame together with the medals. Some quite superb displays have been made in this way.

Remember that display is part of the pleasure of collecting medals and in the final analysis the collector can show his items in the manner that pleases him most. Recently, special holders for medals have been produced, similar to those for coins, and these are rapidly becoming popular.

Appendix I

BARS ISSUED FOR THE NAVAL GENERAL
SERVICE MEDAL 1793–1840
(*Abbreviation wh. stands for with*)

Inscription on Medal	Date on Medal	Bars Issued
Nymphe	*18 June 1793*	4
Crescent	*20 October 1793*	12
Zebra	*7 March 1794*	2
Carysfort	*29 May 1794*	none
(Various ships)	*1 June 1794*	580
Romney	*17 June 1794*	3
Blanche	*4 January 1795*	5
Lively	*13 March 1795*	3
	14 March 1795	114

(Vice-Admiral Hotham with 22 ships engaged the French fleet and captured two prizes)

Astraea	*10 April 1795*	3
Thetis	*17 May 1795*	3
Hussar	*17 May 1795*	1

(Both *Thetis* and *Hussar* for capture of *La Raison* and *Prévoyant*)

Mosquito	*9 June 1795*	none

(The award was not made because shortly after the action the *Mosquito* was lost with all hands)

	17 June 1795	38

(Seven British ships under Cornwallis repulsed a large French fleet)

	23 June 1795	201

(29 ships engaged in major action which captured several French ships, including *Formidable* (renamed *Belleisle*), *Tigre* and recapture of *Alexander*)

Dido	*24 June 1795*	1
Lowestoft	*24 June 1795*	6
Spider	*25 August 1795*	1
Port Spergui	*17 March 1796*	4

(For destroying the gun batteries at Port Spergui in a fiercely-fought engagement)

Indefatigable	*20 April 1796*	6

(Capture of *Virginia*)

Unicorn	*8 June 1796*	4
Santa Margarita	*8 June 1796*	3

Inscription on Medal	Date on Medal	Bars Issued
Southampton	9 June 1796	4
Dryad	13 June 1796	7
(Capture of French ship—renamed *Amelia* in British fleet)		
Terpsichore	13 October 1796	3
Lapwing	3 December 1796	2
Minerva	19 December 1796	5
Blanche	19 December 1796	2
Indefatigable	13 January 1797	8
Amazon	13 January 1797	6
(*Amazon* went aground and her ship's company was taken prisoner)		
St Vincent	14 February 1797	363
(Major engagement with Spanish fleet, 23 British ships took part)		
San Fiorenzo	8 March 1797	7
Nymphe	8 March 1797	6
Camperdown	11 October 1797	336
(Defeat of Dutch fleet by Admiral Duncan)		
Phoebe	21 December 1797	7
(Capture of *Nereide*)		
Mars	21 April 1798	26
Isle St Marcou	6 May 1798	3
Lion	15 July 1798	21
(Capture of *Santa Dorotea*)		
Nile	1 August 1798	351
(Fifteen British ships engaged)		
Espoir	7 August 1798	1
(Capture of pirate ship *La Guria*)	12 October 1798	81
(Eight ships engaged)		
Fisgard	20 October 1799	9
Sybille	28 February 1799	12
(Scots Brigade taking passage in *Sybille* took part)		
Telegraph	18 March 1799	none
Acre	30 May 1799	42
Schiermonikoog	12 August 1799	10
Arrow	13 September 1799	2
Wolverine	13 September 1799	
Surprise/Hermione	25 October 1799	7
(Recapture of *Hermione*)		
Speedy	6 November 1799	3
(Convoy defence against Spanish gunboats)		
Courier	22 November 1799	3
Viper	26 December 1799	2
Fairy	5 February 1800	4

Inscription on Medal	Date on Medal	Bars Issued
Harpy	*5 February 1800*	4
(Capture of *Pallas*—renamed HMS *Pique*)		
Peterel	*21 March 1800*	2
Penelope	*30 March 1800*	11
Vinciego	*30 March 1800*	2
Capture of the Desirée	*8 July 1800*	25
(Eighteen ships engaged, capture of French ship *Desirée*)		
Seine	*20 August 1800*	8
Phoebe	*19 February 1801*	7
Egypt	*1801*	511
(Fleet service off Egypt by 117 ships)		
Copenhagen	*1801*	540
Speedy	*6 May 1801*	7
Gut of Gibraltar	*12 July 1801*	152
(Major action with French and Spanish warships at Gibraltar Gut. The 74-gun *St Antonio* was captured)		
Sylph	*28 September 1801*	2
Pasley	*28 October 1801*	4
Scorpion	*31 March 1804*	4
Beaver	*31 March 1804*	none
Centurion	*18 September 1804*	11
Arrow	*3 February 1805*	8
Acheron	*3 February 1805*	2
(*Arrow* and *Acheron* defended 28 merchant ships from French attack)		
San Fiorenzo	*14 February 1805*	12
Phoenix	*10 August 1805*	22
(Capture of *Didon*)		
Trafalgar	*1805*	1,710
(33 British ships led by Lord Nelson in HMS *Victory*)		
	4 November 1805	298
(Capture of four French warships)		
St Domingo	*1806*	410
(Eleven British ships involved)		
Amazon	*13 March 1806*	27
London	*13 March 1806*	30
Pique	*26 March 1908*	7
Sirius	*17 April 1806*	12
Blanche	*19 July 1806*	23
Arethusa	*23 August 1806*	9
Anson	*23 August 1806*	8
Curaçao	*1 January 1807*	67
(Capture of Curaçao)		

Inscription on Medal	Date on Medal	Bars Issued
Pickle	3 January 1807	1
Hydra	6 August 1807	11
(Attack on Bergur Harbour batteries and capture of three ships)		
Comus	15 August 1807	10
(Capture of Danish frigate)		
Louisa	28 October 1807	1
Carrier	4 November 1807	1
Ann	24 November 1807	none
Sapphò	2 March 1808	5
San Fiorenzo	8 March 1808	16
(A monument to Captain Hardinge, killed in the battle, is in St Paul's Cathedral)		
Emerald	13 March 1808	12
Childers	14 March 1808	4
Nassau	22 March 1808	37
Stately	22 March 1808	32
Off Rota	4 April 1808	19
Grasshopper	24 April 1808	7
Rapid	24 April 1808	1
Redwing	7 May 1808	7
Virginie	19 May 1808	23
Redwing	31 May 1808	5
(Attack on Tarita battery near Cape Trafalgar)		
Seahorse wh. Badere Zaffer	6 July 1808	35
Comet	11 August 1808	5
Centaur	26 August 1808	40
Implacable	26 August 1808	45
(Centaur and Implacable engaged Russian fleet)		
Cruizer	1 November 1808	4
(Defeat of Danish flotilla at Gothenburg)		
Amethyst wh. Thetis	10 November 1808	37
Off The Pearl Rock	13 December 1808	16
Onyx	1 January 1809	6
Confiance	14 January 1808	8
Martinique	1809	500
(Capture of Martinique)		
Horatio	10 February 1809	16
Supérieure	10 February 1809	2
(Both above involved in capture of Junon which was added to British fleet)		
Amethyst	5 April 1809	28

Inscription on Medal	Date on Medal	Bars Issued
Basque Roads	*12 April 1809*	646
(Sea battle of Basque Roads—35 ships)		
Pompée	*17 June 1809*	22
Castor	*17 June 1809*	7
Recruit	*17 June 1809*	5
(Although bars show 'June', action was fought on April 17)		
Cyane	*25/27 June 1809*	5
L'Espoir	*25/27 June 1809*	5
Bonne Citoyenne		
with Furieuse	*6 July 1809*	12
Diana	*11 September 1809*	5
Anse-le-Barque	*18 December 1809*	42
Cherokée	*10 January 1810*	4
Scorpion	*12 January 1810*	7
Guadeloupe	*January/February 1810*	500
(Capture of Guadeloupe, 50 ships involved)		
Thistle	*10 February 1810*	none
Surly	*24 April 1810*	3
Firm	*24 April 1810*	none
Sylvia	*26 April 1810*	1
Spartan	*3 May 1810*	33
Royalist	*May/June 1810*	3
Amanthea	*25 July 1810*	29
Banda Neira	*9 August 1810*	69
Boadicea	*18 September 1810*	18
Otter	*18 September 1810*	8
Staunch	*18 September 1810*	2
Briseis	*14 October 1810*	2
Lissa	*13 March 1811*	130
(Four ships engaged)		
Anholt	*27 March 1811*	46
(Defence of Anholt Island against Danish forces)		
Arrow	*6 April 1811*	none
Off Tamatave	*20 May 1811*	79
Hawke	*18 August 1811*	6
Java	*September 1811*	695
(Capture of *Java*—25 ships engaged)		
Skylark	*11 November 1811*	3
Locust	*11 November 1811*	2
Pelagosa	*29 November 1811*	67
Victorious wh. Rivoli	*22 February 1812*	68
Weasel	*22 February 1812*	6

(Victorious suffered 27 dead and nearly 100 wounded, in capturing *Rivoli*. *Weasel* had no casualties)

Inscription on Medal	Date on Medal	Bars Issued
Rosario	*27 March 1812*	8
Griffon	*27 March 1812*	3
Northumberland	*22 May 1812*	64
Growler	*22 May 1812*	3
Magala	*29 May 1812*	17
(Capture of two French privateers)		
Off Mardoe	*6 July 1812*	50
Sealark	*21 July 1812*	4
Royalist	*29 December 1812*	3
Weasel	*22 April 1813*	5
(Defeat of six French gunboats)		
Shannon with Chesapeake	*1 June 1813*	48
Pelican	*14 August 1813*	4
(Capture of American brig *Argus*)		
St Sebastian	*August/September 1813*	292
Thunder	*9 October 1813*	8
Gluckstadt	*5 January 1814*	49
(Capture of fortress of Gluckstadt)		
Venerable	*16 January 1814*	45
Cyane	*16 January 1814*	7
Eurotas	*25 February 1814*	34
Hebrus wh. L'Etoile	*27 March 1814*	42
Phoebe	*28 March 1814*	28
Cherub	*28 March 1814*	10
(Capture of two American frigates by *Phoebe* and *Cherub*)		
The Potomac	*17 August 1814*	111
(Destruction of ships at Potomac by eight British ships)		
Endymion with President	*15 January 1815*	63
(Capture of American frigate)		
Gaieta	*24 July 1814*	89
Algiers	*27 August 1816*	1,362
(Major battle at Algiers, 22 British ships)		
Navarino	*20 October 1827*	1,137
(Eleven British ships)		
Syria	*November 1840*	7,000
(Capture of Acre and engagements on Syrian coast—32 British ships involved)		

Appendix II

USEFUL BOOKS

ABRAHAM, IRWIN R. *US Merchant Marine Decorations and Awards 1966, Army Officers Awards, Napoleonic Period.*
AMERY, L. S. (Editor). *The Times History of the War in South Africa, 1899–1900.*
BABIN, L. L. *Foreign War Medals, Orders, Decorations.*
  Japanese War Medals, Orders, Decorations.
  Nazi War Medals, Orders and Decorations.
BELDON, B. L. *United States War Medals.* London, 1961.
CARTER, THOS. *Medals of the British Army and how they were won.* London, 1861.
EGGENBERGER, D. *A Dictionary of Battles from 1479 BC to the present.* 1967.
FOSTER, K. O. N. *The Military General Service Medal, 1793–1814.*
GORDON, MAJOR L. L. *British Orders and Awards.* Stafford, 1959.
  British Battles and Medals, 1950.
IRWIN, D. HASTINGS. *War Medals and Decorations,* London, 1890.
JAMES W. *The Naval History of Great Britain, from the declaration of war by France in 1793 to the accession of George IV.* London, 1902.
JENKINS, J. *Naval Achievements of Great Britain.*
JOHNSON, S. C. *The Medal Collector.* London, 1921.
JOSLIN, E. C. *The Standard Catalogue of British Orders, Decorations and Medals.* Spink, 1969.
KERR, W. J. W., (Major). *Notes on War Medals, 1794–1840.*
LONG, W. H. *Medals of the British Navy.* London, 1895.
ADMIRAL THE MARQUESS OF MILFORD HAVEN. *British Naval Medals: Commemorative Medals, Naval Rewards, War Medals, Naval Tokens, Portrait Medallions, Life-Saving Medals, Engraved Pieces, etc.* London, 1919.
MAYO, J. H. *Medals and Decorations of the British Army and Navy.* London, 1897. 2 vols.
POULSOM, N. W. (Major). *The White Ribbon. A medallic record of British Polar Expeditions.*

PURVES, A. A. *Orders, Decorations and Medals, a select bibliography. Some Notes on War Medals*, London, 1958.

ROSS, S. C. *Collectors' Guide to the Military Badges, Medals and Decorations of the Third Reich.*

SANDWICH (Earl of). *British and Foreign Medals Relating to Naval and Maritime Affairs.* HMSO 1937.

SMYTH, BRIGADIER THE RT HON SIR JOHN. *The Story of the George Cross.*

TANCRED, GEORGE. *Historical Record of Medals Conferred on the British Navy, Army and Auxiliary Forces.* London, 1891.

TAPRELL-DORLING, H. (Commander). *Ribbons and Medals, Naval, Military, Air Force and Civil.* 1916.

WERLICH, ROBERT. *Orders and Decorations of all Nations, ancient, civil and military.*

Appendix III

GLOSSARY OF TERMS

ASSEGAIS. Spears often used on medals for campaigns against natives.

BAR (OR CLASP). Used to indicate the detachable metal bar or bars which are found on medals giving the names of various actions, campaigns, etc.

CARTOUCHE. Scroll ornament found on many medal suspenders and on some bars.

COLLAR. Part of an Order worn round the collar. Orders like the Most Noble Order of the Garter comprise: Star, Sash Badge, Collar, Collar Badge, Garter.

EXERGUE (EX). The segment of a medal divided from the remainder by a line near the bottom of the medal—as on the China 1900 Medal.

FIELD. The area of a medal not occupied by the exergue or the device.

FLAN. The blank metal cut to the shape of the medal but unstamped.

GROUP. Medals awarded to a particular person, which may cover several wars are referred to as a 'Group'.

MOIRÉ. Clouded appearance like watered silk found on some ribbons.

MOUNTED (MTD). A group of medals prepared for wearing.

NAMED. Indicates that the medal bears the name of the recipient on the edge. Not all medals were issued named.

NATIVE MEDALS. Awards to natives are usually worth less than those to Europeans because of the difficulty of tracing them on medal rolls.

RIBBON. Every medal has a distinctive coloured ribbon of silk fabric.

SUSPENDER. Method of mounting. Most medals have swivel suspenders, but some, like the Waterloo Medal, were issued with ring suspenders.

INDEX

Printed in the United Kingdom
by Lightning Source UK Ltd.
93381